Rethinking Race

Rethinking Race

Franz Boas and His Contemporaries

Vernon J. Williams Jr.

THE UNIVERSITY PRESS OF KENTUCKY

Editorial and Sales Offices: The University Press of Kentucky
663 South Limestone Street, Lexington, Kentucky 40508-4008

Library of Congress Catalog-in-Publication Data

Williams, Vernon J.
    Rethinking race : Franz Boas and his contemporaries / Vernon J.
Williams, Jr.
    p. cm.
    Includes bibliographic references (p.   ) and index.
    ISBN 0-8131-1963-4 (acid-free recycled paper).—ISBN 0-8131-
0873-x (pbk: acid-free recycled paper)
    1. Boas, Franz, 1858–1942. 2. Anthropologists—United States—
Biography. 3. Anthropologists—United States—Attitudes.
4. Physical anthropology—United States—History. 5. Racism—United
States—History. 6. Afro-Americans—Public opinions. 7. Public
opinion—United States. 8. United States—Race relations.
I. Title.
GN21.B56W55   1996
305.8'96073—dc20   95–34914

To
the memory of
my uncle
Judge Francis Williams
and
my major professor
William G. McLoughlin

Contents

Preface

More than a decade ago I read Alphonso Pinkney's *The Myth of Progress*; that slim volume occasioned the writing of this book during the years that followed. I had just completed a manuscript that extolled the triumph of colorblind egalitarianism in the American social sciences during the years before 1930. I had nevertheless suggested in that same work that the social sciences had failed miserably after that date at resolving the issues revolving around the problem of the redistribution of wealth and power in the United States. Pinkney's work increased my awareness of the extent of the Reagan administration's attempts to discipline the African American poor (blacks made up one-third to one-half of the people affected by programs that the president wanted to cut). I knew from experience that Reagan's declarations were the side effects of an augmenting yet bogus conservatism and racism that had swept the United States since the late 1970s. As a consequence, this book, which may be seen as an extension of my earlier work, is an attempt to reaffirm yet critically assess the rich, colorblind egalitarian traditions in the American social scientific disciplines. In short, I have attempted to describe and analyze the ideas of persons who provided, in a time comparable to our own, the bases of a sophisticated discussion of race and race relations.

Several scholars read this work at its various sequences of development. I offer my sincere thanks to George M. Fredrickson, Leonard Harris, Nancy L. Grant, Wilson J. Moses, Nell I. Painter, and Amritjit Singh. My good colleague Harold D. Woodman and the head of my department, John J. Contreni, have provided strong and steady support over the years at Purdue University. For needed financial support during this period I am indebted to Boston University, the American Council of Learned Societies, and Purdue University. The strong support of all my peers and these institutions makes it possible to confess that whatever errors of fact or interpretation the book contains are attributable solely to the frailty of the author.

Introduction

For more than two generations Franz Uri Boas—thanks primarily to the yeomanlike work of several historians and historically minded social scientists—has assumed a gargantuan stature in intellectual history because of his pioneering role in initiating the antiracist creed in American social science. In his attempts to foster the uplift of African Americans, Boas reacted against the dominant discourse on race and sought to modify the biologistic paradigm that had evolved since the publication of Charles Darwin's *Origin of Species* in 1859. Nevertheless, it must be remembered that he was firmly anchored in his own times when he discussed the relative intellectual capabilities of blacks and whites: Boas believed that because of a supposedly defective ancestry that had resulted in purportedly smaller brain sizes and cranial cavities, blacks were a little inferior—on average—to whites in intelligence. Yet despite this reservation he argued vociferously that the variability of black intelligence precluded the justification of blatant forms of blanket discrimination in the marketplace. For Boas, persons who were black were to be treated as individuals. There was, in other words, no sufficient justification for excluding individual blacks from participating, as much as their capacities allowed, in the community or nation-state. Thus, despite his often ambivalent stance on the issue of the defective ancestry of blacks, Boas offered as one explanation for the low status of blacks in the United States the persistence of Euro-American prejudice. In so doing, he influenced poignantly many educated whites and blacks.

Yet the youthful Boas was also aware of the obstacles to a truly liberating triumph of antiracist attitudes and behavior in the United States, obstacles posed not only by the obdurateness of Euro-Americans' prejudicial attitudes and discriminatory behavior but also by the corresponding fragility of African American high culture. To combat these, he discredited the Euro-American myth that the racial inferiority of Negroes was attributable to their African ancestry by unveiling their glorious past in Africa. At the same time, he attempted to use his evidence of African achievements to enhance the image that African American intellectuals and leaders conveyed of their people. Ironically, however, Boas not only sharpened the African

American intelligentsia's revulsion against Euro-American racism but also, unwittingly, nurtured their belief in distinct, hierarchical attributes in reference to the African past. This tendency resulted in the emergence of various chauvinistic Afrocentric theories of history that have persisted to this day.

Boas responded to the dominant discourse on race in three distinct ways. First, he utilized the tools of anthropometry to generate new facts on which antiracist claims could be based. Second, he used scientific reasoning to question racist explanations of the facts. Third, he drew on both physical and cultural anthropology to remove the racial markers by relabeling supposedly "peculiar" racial traits as universal human traits.[1]

These elicited a variety of responses among the African American intelligentsia. On the one hand, there was a direct monocausal relation to the rise of chauvinistic thinking among blacks. On the other hand, he provided the style of thought that influenced the young generation of antiracist African American social scientists who rose to prominence after 1930.

Unlike Boas, who thought science was a universal, purely empirical form of knowledge, W.E.B. Du Bois—because of the tremendous tension between his elitist and scientific values and his desire to find a solution to the problem of ethnic solidarity among his oppressed brethren—from 1897 to 1915, vacillated between racial chauvinism in reference to the cultural background of African Americans and scientism in reference to their socioeconomic status. Like Boas, however, he too still influences present-day thought on Afrocentrism and the debate concerning race and class.

Unlike Du Bois, Booker T. Washington—the only figure discussed here who was not a social scientist—acted as a symbol of the aspirations of the freedmen. From 1895, when he reached national prominence, until 1901 he identified with the moderate liberal element in the dominant discourse but also used the racial chauvinistic myth of the African American as "loyal, suffering servant" in an attempt to lure capital to his program of gradual uplift through industrial education. From 1901 until 1909 the "Tuskegee wizard" grudgingly moved from identification with antiblack stereotypes—thanks to the influence of his ghostwriters and some of the most progressive voices in the discourse of race—to scientism and, as he became more involved in African affairs, to racial chauvinistic thinking in reference to Africa.

Robert E. Park, the lone Anglo-American extensively treated here, between 1905 and 1913 both contributed to the Washingtonian myths of race relations and challenged scientific racist data concerning the socioeconomic status of blacks. Later, during his tenure at the University of Chicago from 1913 to 1932, he occasionally relapsed into racial stereotyping, but under the influence of Boas and the "Great Migration" he changed his analysis of race, race relations, and prejudice. Finally, during the years 1937 to 1939, under the obvious impact of black progress and his travels abroad, he adopted an "alternative ideology," defined by Nancy Stepan and Sander Gilman as "a radically different world view, with different perceptions of reality, goals and points of reference."[2]

This study relies on both the published work and the correspondence of Franz Boas, Robert E. Park, Booker T. Washington, W.E.B. Du Bois, George Washington Ellis, and Monroe Nathan Work. Through their writings one can trace the tensions that were commonplace at the beginning of the twentieth century for both Euro-Americans and African Americans. I should stress that although the book is chiefly an exercise in the history of ideas, I also pay close attention to the demographic shift of numerous African Americans from the South to the urban-industrial North and to the relevant biographical background of each figure. Perhaps this examination of scientific and political conflicts will enable us to understand why social and cultural determinism—despite the opposition of social biologists and some prominent psychologists—has been the dominant position of leading scholars on race. Put another way, learning the hows and whys of the transition from the myth of African primitivism to the concept of African equipotentiality, from the myth of a homogeneous African American race to the recognition of increasingly intertwined racial status and class, may enable us to understand why current debates assume such volatility.

1

Franz Uri Boas's Paradox

Since the 1950s, historians and historically minded social scientists have celebrated the monumental role that Franz Uri Boas played in eviscerating the racist world view that prevailed in the American social sciences during the years before 1930.[1] Nevertheless, between 1894 and 1938, when Boas addressed the issue of the capabilities of African Americans, his writing exhibited contradictions between his commitment to science and his commitment to the values of his liberal ideology. Reflecting on Boas's life and career up to 1938, his family background and ethnicity, his scientific training, the historical context, and the controversies over the condition and destiny of African Americans, we should be neither surprised that Boas's writings were contradictory nor dismayed that he experienced extreme futility in reconciling the paradoxical elements of his thought.

Despite concurring in the opinion that Boas's thought in reference to the character and capabilities of African Americans was ambiguous or equivocal, some scholars nevertheless argue that his overall tendency was to subordinate racial explanations of man, culture, and society to cultural and social explanations. As a result, these scholars have passed on a legacy of Boas that emphasizes his progressive, egalitarian outlook.[2]

It is just as reasonable to argue that Boas—caught between the social Darwinism of the late nineteenth century and the nascent cultural and social determinism that he was initiating in anthropology during the first two decades of the twentieth century—was (though to a lesser extent than most scholars of his generation) a prisoner of his times. Thus, while it is true that Boas's antiracist stance before 1930 was forward-looking, it is also true that he debated within the essentialist terms laid down by the staunch racists of previous generations and his own, which muted his affirmation of African American equipotentiality. And although it would be a mistake to go so far as to argue—as one of his most perceptive critics did in 1926[3]— that Boas's position on race was static and placated all factions in the American social science community, it is clear that as late as 1938 his thought was marked by the contradiction between the assumptions of physical anthropology and his liberal values.

It should be noted, however, that Boas cannot be labeled a racist as the term is commonly understood. George M. Fredrickson, whose latest definition of racism attempts to be "broad enough to take account of contemporary usage and also covers past discriminatory practices that were not motivated or justified by classic racist doctrine," states that racism is "an ethnic group's assertion or maintenance of a privileged and protected status vis-à-vis members of another group or groups who are thought, because of defective ancestry, to possess a set of socially-relevant characteristics that disqualify them from full membership in a community or citizenship in a nation-state."[4] Boas never asserted or advocated that Euro-Americans should maintain "a privileged and protected status" vis-à-vis African Americans, but on the issue of the "defective ancestry" of African Americans his statements were ambiguous. Yet even when he took the alleged defects into account, he did not view them as sufficiently significant to justify the exclusion of African Americans from the community of scholars or from citizenship in the nation-state. In fact, though harboring doubts about the eventual achievement of a biracial egalitarian society, Boas trained, corresponded, and was actively involved with blacks in reform movements based on the belief that African Americans *should* be assimilated. Thus, despite the confines of his period, Boas was a prisoner there to a lesser extent than most other white scholars: he not only helped lay the foundation of Afrocentrism and multiculturalism; he defined the parameters of the current controversy concerning the saliency of "race," "culture," or "class" as the chief determinant of African Americans' life chances.

Boas's changing thought on African Americans is marked at one end by his first extended conceptualization of the "Negro Problem" in an address titled "Human Faculty as Determined by Race" (published in 1894) and at the other by his extended discussion of African Americans in the last edition of *The Mind of Primitive Man* (published in 1938). It seeks to substantiate three arguments. First, Boas emerged as an enlightened apostle of antiracism for our times only after he had virtually nullified the significance of anthropometric measurements in his assessment of the capabilities of African Americans. Nevertheless, as late as 1915, his racial vision had severe limitations. His attempts to infer the capabilities of African Americans led him to conclude that there might be slight differences in the hereditary aptitudes of blacks and whites.

Second, Boas's analysis of prejudice and his particularistic, rational scientific approach to Africans led him to conclude further that discrimination was the salient variable in American race relations. Indeed, he attacked the problems of prejudice and argued that individual merit, not race, should determine what class position individual blacks should attain in American society.

Despite the schisms in Boas's writing on race up until 1938, his positions on race were dynamic: they evolved. He was always conscious of the growing impact of African Americans upon the nation's economic, social, and cultural life and conscious also of the augmenting of anti-Semitism in his environment. Thus, one of the most obvious findings of my research is the conflict between science and ideology in the thought of Boas, an adherent of a naturalistic world view. As new, empirically verifiable data was uncovered by other scholars, his viewpoint in reference to the condition and destiny of African Americans changed on some issues but remained intact on others. This is not to say that the issues were strictly scientific and not political but to suggest that Boas's political awakening and empirical research were mutually reinforcing. That is, "political beliefs" were as salient as "scientific commitments" in countering the claims of overt racists.

After 1915 Boas not only used the liberal environmentalist argument to dispel the myth of "racial hereditary characteristics" but also acted as adviser to Melville Herskovits, Otto Klineberg, Ruth Benedict, Zora Neale Hurston, Margaret Mead, and Ashley Montagu. These were persons who built on and disseminated the Boasian perspectives on the capabilities of African Americans, on prejudice, and on the achievements of Africans—not only in physical anthropology, cultural anthropology, and literature but also in the broad public arena from the 1910s to the 1960s. Furthermore, Boas transformed the thought of members of the African American intelligentsia, such as Booker T. Washington, W.E.B. Du Bois, Monroe N. Work, George W. Ellis, Carter G. Woodson, George E. Haynes, Alain LeRoy Locke, Charles S. Johnson, Charles H. Thompson, and Abram Harris. Indeed, "it was in the area of race," as Marshall Hyatt has concluded, "that Boas had his greatest impact on American and on future intellectual thought."[5]

Put simply, Boas—albeit grudgingly—attempted to extricate race relations theory from *most* of the racist assumptions of late nineteenth-century social science. Once he had established that white prejudice was the major obstacle to black progress, rather than assumed innate racial traits, it became exceedingly difficult for anthropology and sociology after 1930 to rationalize the caste-like system in the United States on the assumed congenital inferiority of people of West and Central African descent. In sum, from what I call the "Boasian paradox"—the contradiction between his philosophical egalitarian sentiments and his recontextualization of traditional European and American physical anthropology—flowed a prescriptive statement: in a just society African Americans in each socioeconomic class should *approximate* (not assume) a distribution proportional to their size in the U.S. population. Thus, despite his imprisonment in the racist paradigm of late nineteenth-century physical anthropology, which stated that blacks were physically different from and somewhat inferior to whites, Boas at times succeeded in qualifying the inferences drawn from the empirical data to suggest that racism had shaky foundations. He thereby first adumbrated the position of modern-day liberals on the issue of the destiny of African Americans in the social order of the United States. Indeed, Boas felt that once they resolved their problem of group identity, African Americans *could* be assimilated.

The father of modern American anthropology was born into a liberal Jewish household in Minden, Westphalia, Germany, on July 9, 1858, a decade following the republican revolutions that had swept Europe, characterized by an emphasis on liberalism and the creation of democratic republican nations. It was clear by Boas's birth date that these had failed. Nevertheless, Boas's parents—his father, Meier, was a successful merchant; his mother, Sophie, was the founder of the first Froebel Kindergarten in Minden—were the close associates of many prominent "forty-eighters" such as Carl Schurz and Abraham Jacobi, who married Sophie's younger sister. Such a setting inculcated in Boas the liberal ideals of the revolution of 1848—ideals to which he held firmly throughout his life. So intense was the fervor for those ideals in the Boas household that his Jewish background had few direct intellectual consequences for the young Franz. Although "raised an orthodox Jew," as Marshall Hyatt has pointed out, Boas later recalled that his religious education "was purely sop for his grandparents, who were orthodox"; his "parents had broken through the shackles of dogma." According to Boas, "My father had retained an emotional affection for the ceremonial of his parental home, without allowing it to influence his intellectual freedom. Thus I was spared the struggle against religious dogma that besets the lives of so many young people." Still, his ethnicity would have a decisive impact on his later anthropology and politics.[6]

As was customary in Germany during this period, Boas attended several universities: Heidelberg, Bonn, and Kiel. At Kiel in 1881 he was awarded the doctorate in physics with a minor field in geography. His dissertation, "Contributions to the Understanding of the Color of Water," sought to determine the intensities of light that struck different kinds of water. Given the problem of subjectivism when he tried to distinguish between slight differences in color, Boas recalled in 1939, the experiments suggested to him that "there are domains of our experience in which the concepts of quantity . . . with which I was accustomed to operate are not applicable."[7] Questions concerning the relativity of experience and the relationship between the physiological and the physical were two major philosophical problems that he would confront in his later anthropological work.

After an uneventful year at Berlin University and another year in the German army, Boas studied and waited for a teaching position in the increasingly conservative and anti-Semitic academic community in Bismarck's Germany. Disappointed, he went to Baffinland in 1883 to write a book on psychophysics, and his field experience among the Eskimos compelled him to change disciplines. Although the transition from physics to ethnology, as George W. Stocking Jr. has demonstrated, "was not abrupt," this experience sowed the seeds of Boas's attempt to understand the laws of human nature some two years later. While working at the Ethnological Museum after his return, he wrote: "It was with feelings of sorrow and regret that I parted from my Arctic friends. I had seen that they enjoy life, and a hard life, as we do; that nature is also beautiful to them; that feelings of friendship also root in the Eskimo heart; that, although the character of their life is so rude as compared to civilized life, the Eskimo is a man as we are; that his feelings, his virtues and his shortcomings are based in human nature, like ours."[8] Boas's ambivalence toward the Eskimos—the tension between his "philosophical egalitarianism" and his cultural chauvinism, which is obvious in this passage—would later be reflected in his statements on African Americans.

Seeking better career opportunities in ethnology, Boas emigrated to the United States in 1887 but suffered tremendous setbacks in his attempts to secure steady employment in Anglo-American-dominated institutions. Virulent anti-Semitism pervaded the nation when Boas entered the country. Jews of German descent, who had begun to be affected by anti-Semitism as early as the 1880s, witnessed a decline in status and narrowed opportunities during the 1890s as direct products of the influx of large numbers of Eastern European Jews since the 1880s. Boas's post as geographical editor of *Science* was not funded in 1888; he was forced to resign a position as a docent in physical anthropology at Clark University in 1892; and he was dismissed from a temporary position as chief assistant of anthropology at the World's Columbian Exposition in Chicago in 1894. Also in 1894, William Rainey Harper, president of the University of Chicago, refused to offer him a professorship, citing his inability to "take direction" as one reason. In 1894, the unemployed Boas was delaying his creditors and mourning the death of his young son.

When Boas delivered his outgoing address as vice-president of Section H of the American Association for the Advancement of Science in Brooklyn, New York, in August 1894, he was expressing liberal convictions that flowed from a world view unique in the United States—convictions that were a direct product of the remnants of liberal ideals in Germany, his scientific training, and his marginal status in the anthropological community. Furthermore, this attack on the racist orthodoxy permeating both

European and American social scientific communities was bound inextricably to both the so-called "Negro problem" of the North and the South and the virulent anti-Semitism that pervaded the nation.

In turn-of-the-century America, Negrophobia pervaded every aspect of the nation's life and was a formidable obstacle to rational discussion of the condition of African Americans. The 1877 reconciliation between North and South had resulted in the subordination of southern blacks by the early 1880s. As a consequence, despite the economic gains made by some blacks, the period from roughly 1890 until 1920 was one of the lowest points in the history of white-black relations in the United States. Indeed, through disenfranchisement, Jim Crow laws, extralegal violence, and the removal of blacks from skilled labor, whites had consolidated their dominance by 1900. In the North these forms of blatant racism had been less extreme, yet prejudice and discrimination had exacerbated the social problems of blacks and stymied their progress there as well. Developments in the race relations of the period were among the most shameful episodes in American history. The level of the discussion of the intellectual capabilities of African Americans was an obstacle that Boas, because of his adherence to physical anthropological background assumptions and his methodological puritanism, had great difficulty surmounting. For the most significant myths espoused in the dominant discourse stated that African Americans were a homogeneous race whose low status in American society was due not just to an instinctive white prejudice but to a defective ancestry that prevented them from contributing to society, or to "the mores" that excluded them from communal life with Euro-Americans.[9]

In the long article called "Human Faculty as Determined by Race" (1894), Boas presented views that George W. Stocking Jr. and Marshall Hyatt have claimed were the genesis of the themes he pursued throughout the rest of his career. Although I concur in Hyatt's argument that Boas's ethnic status was one of the primary motivating forces behind his attacks on anti-Negro prejudice, it should be noted that "Human Faculty" contains sections infused with Boas's own bigotry toward African Americans. Rationalizing that bigotry in 1968, Stocking wrote: "Given the atmospheric pervasiveness of the idea of European racial superiority, it is hardly surprising that Boas wrote as a skeptic of received belief rather than a staunch advocate of racial equipotentiality. Despite his basic liberal humanitarian outlook, he was a white-skinned European writing for other white-skinned Europeans at the turn of century, and he was a physical anthropologist to boot."[10] In 1974, however, Stocking pointed out that "one is struck by the limits of Boas' critique in 1894."[11] Still, although aware of Boas's limitations, Stocking has suggested that they in no way detract from the fundamental Boasian stance on race.

But Boas's analysis of the physical characteristics of blacks and his "men of high genius" hypothesis, which can be found in his work as late as 1938, contain several biases that detract from his stature as a philosophical egalitarian. His assessments of racial determinist arguments in the various branches of the social sciences were divided in 1894. On the one hand, he demonstrated the primacy of cultural determinants in accounting for historical achievements and the psychological makeup of different races. On the other hand, he conceded to racists by insisting on the relevance of physical anthropological assumptions of the direct relation between intelligence and brain weight or cranial capacity; he even thought that bodily form might have certain influences on the psychological makeup of races. This schism between the values of cultural determinism and the values of racial determinism, a direct product of his methodological rigor, was the major weakness in his philosophical position on race. Although Boas's sentiments resonated with his emphasis on cultural determinism, he still could not reconcile those sentiments with physical anthropological assumptions about racial differences. The tension is evident in his analysis of racial determinism from the historical and physical anthropological perspectives.

From the historical perspective, the young Boas attacked the paradigm of the proponents of the comparative method. By assuming a direct relationship between a race's achievements and the intellectual capacities of its members, the evolutionary anthropologists had essentially confounded achievement with an aptitude for achievement. Similarly, they judged any deviation from the white type as "a characteristic feature of a lower type." Boas insisted that the superiority of Western civilization could be accounted for on grounds other than those suggesting the superiority of the white race's mental faculty. He argued that other races such as the Indians of Peru and Central America had evolved civilizations similar to that in which European civilization had its origins. European civilization, however—favored by the "common physical appearance, contiguity of habitat and modern differences in modes of manufacture" of its inhabitants—had spread rapidly. When it came into contact with races outside its domain, assimilation of nonwhites was difficult because of "striking differences of racial types, the preceding and the greater advance in civilization." The advocates of northern and western European superiority, he stressed, had ignored the fact that their civilization, which arose under favorable circumstances, had "cut short" the development of non-European civilization "without regard to the people whom it was developing." The evolutionists' historical explanation of the low status of nonwhites was wrong because "historical events rather than race appear to have been much more potent in leading races to civilization than their faculty, and it follows

[that] the achievements of races do not warrant us to assume that one race is more highly gifted than the others."[12]

Boas's criticism of the evolutionists had exposed the ethnocentric fallacy of ranking nonwhite societies according to the characteristics they shared with European and American civilizations, but his evaluation of racial intellectual differences from the physical anthropological framework was infused with concessions to staunch racists. In the 1880s and early 1890s he had been influenced significantly by the works of prominent Continental physical anthropologists such as Paul Broca and Paul Topinard, and directly by Rudolph Virchow, whom he had met at the meetings of the Berlin Anthropological Society in 1882. Furthermore, throughout his career Boas was certain that physical anthropological data could clarify important ethnological questions.[13] He worked within the essentialist framework developed by Broca, the father of modern physical anthropology, who wrote in 1873 that a table he had constructed "shows that West Africans have a cranial capacity about 100 c.c. less than the European races. To this figure we may add the following: Caffirs, Nubians, Tasmanians, Hottentots, Australians. These examples are sufficient to prove that if the volume of the cranium does not play a decisive role in the ranking of the races it nevertheless has a very real importance."[14]

Similarly, Boas speculated, in the early jargon of the discipline, "It would seem that the greater the central nervous system, the higher the faculty of the race and the greater its aptitude to mental achievement." Two methods were useful in determining the size of the central nervous system, he said: one could measure either the weight of the brain (which provided the most "accurate results") or the size of the cranial cavity. He conceded that both the brain weight and cranial cavities of whites were, on the average, larger than those of "most other races, particularly . . . the negroes."[15] His conclusions were not new. As early as the 1840s the "American school" of anthropology, of which Samuel George Morton, Josiah C. Nott, and George R. Gliddon were among the members, had based a major part of its proslavery defense on the comparative measurements of the cranial cavities of blacks and whites.[16]

Despite Boas's physical anthropological assumptions, however, he exercised considerable restraint in interpreting data that were based solely on the relatively simple mathematical techniques of means, medians, and percentiles. On a visit to England in 1889 he had become acquainted with Sir Francis Galton and appropriated the eugenicist's science of biometrics to demonstrate that the "frequency distribution" of the cranial cavities of blacks and whites overlapped. Topinard's measurements, he pointed out, revealed that 55 percent of Europeans and 58 percent of "African negroes" had cavities in the range of 1,450 to 1,650 cubic centimeters but that 50 percent of whites and only 27 percent of blacks were in the range greater than 1,550 cubic centimeters. His inference: "We might, therefore, anticipate a lack of men of high genius [among blacks] but should not anticipate any lack of faculty among the great mass of negroes living among whites and enjoying the leadership of the best men of the race."[17]

The statement reflects obvious tension between liberal humanitarian sentiments and the ideas of racism. On the one hand, he implied strongly that blacks would produce proportionately fewer men capable of shaping either the nation's or the world's higher affairs; on the other hand, he was arguing for the significance of individual differences regardless of a person's race. Not *all* blacks, in other words, were intellectually inferior to *all* whites, though disproportionately few had the mental faculty requisite to shape the course of history.

Indeed, in 1894 there was slight distinction between the position of Boas and that of ethnocentricists in institutions dominated by persons of British ancestry. Consider the statements regarding the apelike physical characteristics of the "negro" made by leading "scientific" authorities on race. The Kentucky-born professor of paleontology at Harvard, Nathaniel S. Shaler, stated in 1890 that the Negro was "nearer to the anthropoid or pre-human ancestry of man." In 1896 Edward D. Cope, a Pennsylvania-born Quaker and professor of geology and mineralogy at the University of Pennsylvania, argued that the Negro was ape-like because of the flat nose, jaws that projected beyond the upper part of the face, the facial angle, "the deficiency of the calf of the leg, and the obliquity of the pelvis." Daniel G. Brinton, a former medical doctor who was appointed professor of linguistics and folklore at the University of Pennsylvania, was typical of northern white supremacists in anthropology: "The adult who retains the more numerous fetal, infantile or simian [characteristics]," he wrote in 1890, "is unquestionably inferior to him whose development has progressed beyond them. . . . Measured by these criteria the European or white race stands at head of the list, the African or negro at its foot."[18] In sum, most European and American physical anthropologists believed that the Negroes were apelike barbarians in their midst whose physiques prevented them from attaining civilization.

In "Human Faculty," Boas clearly manifested the arrogance of his contemporaries:

> We found that the face of the negro as compared to the skull is larger than that of the American [Indian], whose face is in turn larger than that of the white. The lower portion of the face assumes larger dimensions. The alveolar arch is pushed forward and thus gains an ap-

pearance which reminds us of the higher apes. There is no denying that this feature is a most constant character of the black races representing a type slightly nearer the animal than the European type. The same may be said of the broadness and flatness of the nose of the negro and of the Mongol; but here again we must call to mind that prognathism, and low broad noses are not entirely absent from the white races, although the more strongly developed forms which are found among negroes do not occur. The variations belonging to both races overlap. We find here at least a few indications which tend to show that the white race differs more from the higher apes than [does] the negro.[19]

Nevertheless, applying the tools of science to all the anthropometric measurements he could obtain on the various races, he concluded: "We have no right to consider one [race] more ape-like than the other."[20] The question of course remains whether Boas, after making such graphic statements about the simian characteristics of Negroes, successfully convinced a male, white-skinned European and American audience of his skepticism.

Boas's "men of high genius" hypothesis was a pitfall from which he was never fully able to extricate himself, and the tenacity with which he held to this conviction demonstrates that one aspect of his views was severely limited by his belief that some racial differences were real. Even in his own day, however, the hypothesis was suspect. Both the anatomist E.A. Spitzka and the sociologist William I. Thomas pointed out that the brain size of eminent whites varied enormously. Furthermore, Thomas asserted in his 1895 article "The Scope and Method of Folk-Psychology," "functionally . . . the importance of the brain has been unduly emphasized by certain anthropologists." The cerebral lobes might be "the seat of consciousness," but "the brain is no more essential to intelligence than is the circulation, or digestion, or the liver. . . . "Intelligence is the mediation of action, and all organs and tissues cooperate in forming an association, are equally important with the brain." As to brain mass, Thomas continued:

> The five heaviest brains recorded by Topinard are those of Tourgenieff (2020 gr.), a day laborer (1925 gr.), a brickmason (1900 gr.), an epileptic (1830 gr.), and the illustrious Cuvier (1830 gr.) French anthropologists have reckoned the average brain-weight as 1360 grammes, and the inferior limit of brain-weight compatible with reason as 1000 grammes. But when their idol Gambetta lately willed them his brain and died, they were mortified to find that it weighed only 1100 grammes-just 100 grammes above the point of imbecility. These facts merely show that preconceptions were wrong, and that anthropology has made itself more scientific in this regard. Gross anatomy of the brain, especially in the hands of surgeons, and fine anatomy, in the hands of neurologists, have established important laws of growth and

of mental pathology, but no anthropologist can venture to say of a series of brains which are male and which female, which Chinese and which German. The whole matter of relation of intelligence to brain-weight, and of the nature and quantity of energy which is a function of this organ, is indeed, fundamentally a question of physiological chemistry. The assumption that capacity for muscular work is in direct proportion to the [muscle] mass is approximately correct; but the assumption that capacity for mental work is in proportion to the mass of nerve substance is a gross error, as anthropologists now very well know. Physiologists are, indeed, compelled to assume a different principle of metabolism in the nerves from that of the muscles, though the nerves have thus far eluded inquiry in this direction.[21]

Yet even though science has confirmed the arguments of Spitzka and Thomas, both men at this juncture were unable to rid themselves of their racial biases and, despite evidence to the contrary, deemed blacks to be intellectually inferior to or temperamentally different from whites.

Boas's 1900 address before the American Folklore Society reflected the tension between his liberal humanitarian sentiments and the evidence from physical anthropology. Willing to pursue the cultural determinist position to some extent, he argued that the mind of primitive man differed from that of civilized man not in its organization, as the advocates of the comparative method had proposed, but rather in the character of experience to which it was exposed. The mental functions—abstraction, inhibition, and choice—could all be found among primitive peoples; thus, there was no justification for the Spencerian argument that primitive peoples occupied a lower evolutionary stage. In the same address, however, Boas retreated to the argument of black inferiority when he confessed: "A number of anatomical facts point to the conclusion that the races of Africa, Australia, and Melanesia are to a certain extent inferior to [those of] Asia, America, and Europe." Still, he did argue that there was "no satisfactory evidence" as to whether differences in the size of the brain were "accompanied by difference in structure."[22]

Boas's ambivalences concerning black capabilities extended also to his discussion of their psychology. The descriptive psychological evidence on which Edward B. Tylor and Herbert Spencer based their generalizations about primitive peoples had suggested that nonwhites were more fickle and passionate and less original than whites, but to Boas, such arguments were not convincing "because causes and effects were so closely interwoven that it is impossible to separate them in a satisfactory manner, and we are always liable to interpret as racial characteristics what is only an effect of social surroundings."[23] Even on that issue, however, Boas infused physical anthro-

The Brain of
General Skobeleff

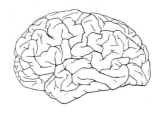

Professor Altmann,
famous anatomist

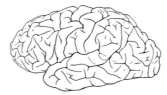

Gambetta

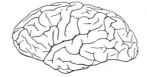

pological assumptions into psychology and immediately genuflected to reactionary beliefs:

> We believe that in the more complicated psychological phenomena no
> specific differences between the higher and lower races can be found.
> By this, however, we do not mean to say no differences exist, . . . only
> that the method of investigation must be different. It does not seem
> probable that the minds of races which show variations in their ana-
> tomical structure should act in exactly the same manner. Differences of
> structure must be accompanied by differences of function, physiolog-
> ical as well as psychological, and as we found clear evidence of differ-
> ences in mental structure between the races, so we must anticipate that
> differences in mental characteristics will be found.[24]

Then, in a feeble attempt to qualify those statements, Boas once again
argued that there were variations in all races: "As all structural differences
are quantitative, we must expect to find mental differences to be of the
same description, and as we found the variation in structure to overlap, so

that many forms are common to individuals of all races, so we may expect that many individuals will not differ in regard to their faculty, while a statistical inquiry embracing the whole race would reveal certain differences."[25]

Between 1894 and 1915 the increasing migration of blacks from the rural areas in the southeastern states to New York City stimulated Boas to take part in reformist activities centering on the condition of the black migrants and compelled him to modify his views concerning the capabilities of blacks. From 1890 to 1910 the black population of New York City almost tripled. By 1910 there were 91,709 blacks in the five boroughs, of whom 60,534 lived in Manhattan and 22,708 in Brooklyn. "The average Negro migrant," Gilbert Osofsky wrote, "obviously found life harsh and difficult. For those who came, however, conditions in the North did offer a measure of self-respect and the possibility for future advancement that was generally denied the Negro in the South."[26] In fact, the net effect of the black migration was to initiate racial violence and antagonism and exacerbate the "social problems" brought about by urbanization. Yet even though recent studies of African American migrations have attempted to demonstrate that the realities of life in the North for most southern African Americans were disappointing, I concur in George M. Fredrickson's argument that turn-of-the-century conditions in the urban-industrial North were more amenable to black progress than those in the South because blacks were subject to less blatant forms of discrimination and were able to exercise their voting rights.[27]

Fortunately, Boas was aware of the need to provide a "scientific" opinion on the "Negro problem." Thanks to an initial appointment as assistant curator at the American Museum of Natural History by his friend Frederic Ward Putnam, he obtained a position as lecturer at Columbia University in 1896 and was tenured in 1899. He joined with progressives— urban reformers such as Mary White Ovington, Victoria Earle Matthews, Frances A. Kellor, and William Lewis Bulkley who were concerned with the welfare of African Americans—and searched for order in a city characterized by disorganization and pathological conditions. Boas and Ovington, who was one of the founders of the National Association for the Advancement of Colored People (NAACP), were members of the Greenwich House Committee on Social Investigation, a moral reform organization to which others from the Columbia University faculty such as Edwin R.A. Seligman, Vladimir Simkhovich, Edward T. Devine, Livingston Farrand, Franklin H. Giddings, and Henry R. Seager belonged. Furthermore, in 1905 Boas published his point of view in *Charities* when that social service magazine devoted an entire issue to the migration of blacks and the consequent social problems. In addition, Boas penned an article for the first issue of *The Crisis*, the organ of the NAACP.[28]

In the 1905 article "The Negro and the Demands of Modern Life," Boas apparently tried to resolve the issues he had raised in 1894 when he argued that blacks would produce proportionately fewer "men of high genius" than whites. Although he once again pointed out that the "average" Negro brain was "smaller than that of other races," and that it was "plausible that certain differences of form of brain exist," he nevertheless cautioned that the data did not conclusively demonstrate differences in intellectual ability. Modifying his 1894 position on the relationship between brain weight and mental ability, Boas argued: "We must remember that individually the correlation . . . is often overshadowed by other causes, and that we find a considerable number of great men with slight brain weight." Yet he was still too committed to physical anthropological assumptions to dismiss them and immediately penned a non sequitor contradicting his suggestion that "causes" other than brain weight might affect mental ability: "We may, therefore, expect less average ability and also, on account of probable anatomical differences, somewhat different mental tendencies." Then, in an attempt to minimize the purported differences between the races, he brought forth the same argument he had used in 1894: "We may, with the same degree of certainty, expect these differences to be small as compared to the total range of variations found in the human species."[29]

Boas attempted to give a favorable impression of African Americans, despite their smaller cranial measurements. In a passage that was a direct attack on segregation in the public schools, he wrote: "There is every reason to believe that the Negro when given the facility and opportunity will be perfectly able to fill the duties of citizenship as well as his white neighbor. It may be that he will not produce as many great men as the white race, and his average achievement will not quite reach the level of the average achievement of the white race, but there will be endless numbers who will do better than the [white] defectives whom we permit to drag down and retard the healthy children of our public schools."[30] Rhetoric aside, Boas was confronted by an irreconcilable dilemma. As a physical anthropologist he adhered to the assumptions of his field, but the foregoing passage reflects the paradox that had been part and parcel of Boasian thought since 1894. Insofar as he thought a black would be "able to fill the duties of citizenship as well as his white neighbor," he was making the case for the full participation of blacks in American life. Yet his formulation of the "approximate" intellectual equality of blacks and whites reveals both his progressive and his reactionary values. To the extent that Boas was arguing for the necessity of taking individual differences into account in assessing a person's capabilities—and therefore his or her intrinsic worth in the marketplace—he was making the case for differentiation in the black class structure. But by suggesting that blacks were only approximately equal to whites, Boas was either consciously or unconsciously providing the rationalization for some discrimination in the economic sector.

Nevertheless, as early as 1905 Boas revealed in his correspondence a healthy skepticism concerning the inferences drawn from anthropometric assessments, basing his objections on the insufficiency of the data. He regarded himself as an empiricist and frequently suggested that the empirical data were inadequate to support conclusions of black inferiority on the basis of racial difference. Writing on October 21, 1905, to Edward T. Devine, a colleague at Columbia and general secretary of the Charity Organization, Boas emphasized "the desirability of collecting more definite information in relation to certain traits of the Negro race that seem of fundamental importance in determining the policy to be pursued towards that race." The problem he thought paramount concerned "the determination of the period of development of the Negro race as compared to the white race." Proponents of Negro inferiority claimed that there was an "early" intellectual "arrest of development of the Negro child," but Boas, who had "gone over available material with some care," found the evidence for that claim "wholly insufficient"; "really the problem must be taken up more." Boas thought he could "definitely solve our problem" if he could "get a trained observer to collect data on stature, weight, size of head, development of nose, time of eruption of teeth (milk teeth and permanent teeth), puberty and senility." Meanwhile, he continued, "I should try to make a test of preliminary cases showing the rapidity of development of practice in Negroes and in whites on some psychological experiment, selecting a test in which influence of school-teaching could count for but little."[31] During this period (as I will show later) Boas thought psychological testing could provide a definitive statement on the relative capabilities of blacks and whites.

He was even more precise about the problems confronting students of race when he wrote on March 15, 1906, to Vladimir G. Simkhovich, a colleague at Columbia and member of the Cooperative Social Settlement Society of the City of New York, in an attempt to gain funds for anthropometric studies.

> The other day we discussed the question of investigations made on the Negroes in America. As stated in our conversation, the fundamental question of the influence of race mixture upon the vitality and ability of the offspring has never been solved. It is generally assumed that the mulatto is inferior, mentally and physically, to either parental race, but all the available material is vitiated by a lack of consideration of the influence of social conditions. This whole question, of course, involves the problem of the mental and physical inferiority of the Negro race, which is not less doubtful than the problem of race mixture.

Both these questions, which are the foundation of our whole policy in regard to the black race, are quite tangible, and with the present development of anthropological methods could easily be taken up and placed on a scientific basis, sufficient to determine the proper policy to be pursued. . . .

(1) Is there an earlier arrest of mental and physical development in the Negro child, as compared with the white child? And, if so, is this arrest due to social causes or to anatomical and physiological conditions?

(2) What is the position of the mulatto child and of the adult mulatto in relation to the two races? Is he an intermediate type, or is there a tendency of reversion towards either race? So that particularly gifted mulattoes have to be considered as reversals of the white race. The question of the physical vigor of the mulatto could be taken up at the same time.[32]

Simkhovich did not fund the project but referred Boas to other possibly sympathetic philanthropists. On October 10, 1906, Boas proposed to Felix Adler, a close associate, a museum whose investigation "would have the most important bearing upon the question of a general policy to be pursued in regard to the negro. . . . The questions that are obscure in reference to this point are innumerable," he stated. We do not know the significance of the slightly different type of organization of the brain. We do not know the laws of growth and of development of the negro race; and all these, taken together, should be investigated, and the result of an unbiased, patient investigation of these problems should be of the very greatest help in all practical problems."[33] In these letters he seemed to be suggesting that physical anthropology had the potential to provide data on which public policy regarding the Negro should be based.

Although Boas assumed a skeptical posture before white persons who were possible sources of funding for his proposed projects on the anthropometry of the Negro and mulatto, he still held a conviction that Negroes were serially inferior to whites. Writing to Rev. James Boddy of Troy, New York, on May 7, 1906, he asserted: "You may be aware that in my opinion the assumption seems justifiable that on the average the mental capacity of the negro may be a little less than that of the white, but that the capacities of the bulk of both races are on the same level." Boas admitted that he could "find neither any history nor any anatomical considerations in proof of any considerable inferiority of the negro race," but always guided by the assumptions of physical anthropology, he conjectured that "it seems of course likely that owing to the differences of anatomical traits, mental differences also exist." Nonetheless, he concluded, "the differences are slight as compared to the variability found in each race."[34]

It should also be noted that Boas's methodological puritanism often prevented him from professing to blacks who sought his expertise that the equipotentiality of blacks was a scientific fact. For example, in response to R.R. Wright Sr., the African American president of Georgia State Industrial College, who asked him to cite "some authorities" that he could "consult upon the ancient history of the African Race, or the Negro in particular," Boas wrote in 1907: "I think you understand my view in regard to the ability of the Negro quite agrees with what you say in your paper. I wish, however, that it were possible to take up a careful study of this subject, and to present the results to our fellow-citizens in a convincing manner. Unfortunately it does not help us that we ourselves have clear convictions in regard to this subject. The reasons for our convictions should be represented in an answerable form, and I believe the only thing that will serve this purpose will be a very painstaking and detailed presentation of the results of studies of African ethnology on the one hand, and of the anatomical features of the central nervous system of the white race and of the negro race on the other."[35] In other words, he exercised extreme caution in expressing his convictions; he thought the need for further research was a prerequisite for making the case against rigid racial determinism.

For Boas, further empirical research was also a prerequisite for scholars who were attempting to make the case for rigid racial differences. In a letter to Richard Watson Gilder of the popular *Century Illustrated Monthly Magazine*, Boas was extremely critical of Robert B. Bean, whose article "The Negro Brain" had appeared in Gilder's magazine in 1906. Bean, a southerner and an anatomist at the University of Virginia, had argued "(1) that the Caucasian brain is heavier than that of the negro, (2) that the relative quantity of white fiber is greater in the Caucasian than in the negro, and (3) that the anterior association center (front end of the brain) and the front end of the corpus callosum are larger in the Caucasian than the negro." The first two arguments suggested that the brain of blacks contained "less gray matter (nerve cells)," which were the "basis of brain power or mental ability," and less "white matter (nerve fibers)," on which the efficiency of the brain" depended.[36] The third argument, which was based on what Stocking has labeled "localization theory," suggested that in whites the frontal lobes—where Bean and other anatomists thought "the highest developed faculties of man, the motor speech-center for the command of languages, will power, the power of self-control, the power of inhibition and perseverance; the ethical and esthetic faculties; and the power of thought in the abstract" were located—were larger than in blacks.[37]

Angered by the fact that Bean's article lacked corroborating data for his three arguments, Boas exclaimed to Gilder: "The mere fact that a paper of this kind should have found a place in a journal of the reputation of *The Century* will give strong support to those who deny the negro equal rights; and from this point of view I think the advance publication of the paper is not just to the cause of the negro."[38] Furthermore, in "The Anthropological Position of the Negro," which appeared in *Van Norden's Magazine* a few months later, Boas attempted to refute Bean by arguing that "the anatomical differences" between blacks and whites "are minute," and "no scientific proof that will stand honest proof . . . would prove the inferiority of the negro race."[39]

Although that statement is atypical of Boas's stance—since he generally refused to express so strong a conviction—by 1909 before reform-minded persons he had begun to minimize the significance of racial intellectual differences between blacks and whites. In his short article for *The Crisis*, after reviewing the data on the size of the Negro brain, he stated that "the existing differences are differences in kind, not in value. This implies that the biological evidence also does not sustain the view . . . so often proposed that the mental power of the one race is higher than that of the other, although their mental qualities show, presumably, differences analogous to the existing anatomical and physiological differences."[40]

Boas's thought at this juncture remained uneven. That same year in an article published in *Science* he stated that there were fundamental differences between whites and blacks: "I do not believe that the negro is, in his physical and mental make-up the same as the European. The anatomical differences are so great that corresponding mental differences are plausible. There may exist differences in character and in the direction of specific aptitudes. There is, however, no proof whatever that these differences signify any appreciable degree of inferiority of the negro, notwithstanding the slightly inferior size, and perhaps lesser complexity of structure, of his brain; for these racial differences are much less than the range of variation found in either race considered by itself."[41] Nevertheless, aware of the scientific doubts about physical anthropological explanations of mental differences, Boas wrote in that same article:

> I think we have reason to be ashamed to confess that the scientific study of these [Negro] questions has never received the support either of our government or of any of our great scientific institutions; and it is hard to understand why we are so indifferent towards a question which is of paramount importance to the welfare of our nation. The anatomy of the American negro is not well known; and, notwithstanding the oft-repeated assertions regarding the hereditary inferiority of the mulatto, we know hardly anything on this subject. If his vitality is lower than that of the full-blooded negro, this may be as much due to social causes as to hereditary causes. Owing to very large numbers of

mulattoes in our country, it would not be a difficult matter to investigate the biological aspects of this question thoroughly; and the importance of the problem demands that this should be done.[42]

In 1911 Boas published *The Mind of Primitive Man*, a book that included excerpts from his previously published essays on race but also contained the most recent data supporting conclusions that Boas had been developing since 1894. It was complete in its refutation of crude racial determinist thinking, complete in its indictment of crude racial prejudice, and cogent in its presentation of the assimilationist arguments.

In a 1912 review of the book, Robert H. Lowie, who had been one of Boas's students, lucidly explicated his mentor's position:

> If, then, participation in a superior culture is not proof of superior endowment, anatomical deviations from the white norm cannot be regarded as evidence of inferiority without begging the question. As a matter of fact, the European stands in certain zoölogical traits closer to the apes than other races, 'while the specifically human development of the red lip is developed most markedly in the Negro" (p. 22). So far as the racial differences in brain weight are concerned, Boas reminds us that the relation between weight and ability is not univocal; thus, the sexual differences within the same race seem to be correlated with differences in quality rather than grade of faculty, and exceptional brain weight is not uniformly coupled with exceptional ability. While thus warning against an overestimation of the correlation between mental faculty and brain development, the author emphatically asserts that some psychological differences must be assumed to be correlated with the anatomical differences, though they may be of a qualitative character. But the variability of the individuals within any one race is so great that no racial differences have hitherto been definitely established and a comparison of white brains with Negro brains leads to the result that the vast majority of individuals of the two series compared coincide. The Negro race may not produce as many minds of exceptional ability as the white race; but so far as its average performance is concerned Boas arrives at the conclusion that there is no evidence for believing in a racial inferiority that would unfit an individual Negro to take his part in modern civilizations.[43]

The culmination of Boas's thought on blacks during the Progressive era, however, was not reached until the publication of his foreword to Mary White Ovington's *Half A Man* in 1915: "Many students of anthropology recognize that no proof can be given of any material inferiority of the Negro race; that without doubt the bulk of the individuals composing the race are equal in mental aptitude to the bulk of our own people; that, although their hereditary aptitude may lie in slightly different directions, it is very improbable that the majority of individuals composing the white race should possess greater ability than the Negro race."[44] In essence, Boas minimized the significance of purported intellectual differences between blacks and whites by stressing that the masses of both races were virtually equal. Nonetheless, he raised a key issue that was far from being resolved at his death in 1942. Were the slight differences in "hereditary aptitude" that he detected socially significant? In other words, what were the implications for the professions and highly skilled trades of slight differences in racial aptitudes? He could not answer these questions, and they continue to be debated to this day.

Despite Boas's admission that it was practically impossible to separate the social and hereditary features of the mental make-up of whites and blacks, he had argued in 1894 that "investigations based on physiological psychology and experimental psychology will allow us to treat the problem in a satisfactory manner." He recommended investigating "the psychical processes of great numbers of individuals of different races who live under similar conditions." That had not been done sufficiently to allow "far-reaching conclusions," but the schools were a place to start. Boas mentioned "that Professor Barnes and Miss Hicks found differences of favorite colors between children of different races and different ages; that attempts have been made to show that the minds of negro children cease to develop sooner than those of white children, although the results are not conclusive. Modest investigation of the senses of simpler mental activities of children will give the first satisfactory answer to the important question of the *extent of racial differences* [emphasis added] of faculty. The schools of our country, particularly those of larger cities, open a vast field for researches of this character."[45]

By the end of the 1910s the efforts of psychologists to investigate the psychical processes had proliferated, but Boas, always the methodological puritan, rejected findings that lacked methodological rigor. He and his students—Melville Herskovits, Margaret Mead, Ashley Montagu, Otto Klineberg—would become the leading adversaries in the fight against the attempt of psychologists to prove black inferiority on the basis of aptitude tests. It is clear from Lowie's explication—as Frank H. Hankins astutely pointed out—that Boas thought "racial differences though real are less extensive and important than popular opinion has heretofore supposed."[46]

The fact that Boas worked within the same essentialist framework as the racists should not detract from the subversiveness of his position on the capabilities of African Americans. The initial response to Boas in anthropology was almost hysterical; Daniel G. Brinton, in his presidential address to the American Association for the Advancement of Science in 1895 asserted: "The black, the brown and red races differ anatomically so much from the white, especially in their splanchnic [visceral] organs, that even with equal cerebral capacity, they could never rival the results by equal efforts."[47] Yet by the early 1900s Boas—thanks to his security at Columbia and his ties to the Smithsonian Institute, the American Association for the Advancement of Science, and the American Ethnological Society—had become a powerful figure in American anthropology. His political domination of the discipline resulted in the triumph of his position within it after 1920.[48]

In the closely allied discipline of sociology the initial responses to the Boasian position on the capabilities of blacks were determined by the ethnic and sectional backgrounds of the partisans, the extent to which they accepted scientific naturalism as a world view, and their perception of the social structural changes that were affecting blacks in the nation.[49] By 1918, however, the Boasian position had triumphed, and the disciple's leading student of race relations, Robert E. Park, summed up the view of the most prominent sociologists: "The question remains where Boas left it when he said that the black was little, if any, inferior to the white man in intellectual capacity and in any case, racial as compared with individual differences were small and relatively unimportant."[50] During the next few decades, sociologists would be among the staunchest supporters of this position.

Despite Boas's adherence to the assumptions of physical anthropology and experimental psychology, he knew that whites determined the status of blacks in the American socioeconomic order and that their attitudes and behavior confined blacks to a low position. Time and again, between 1894 and 1915 Boas identified the racial prejudice of white Americans as the primary determinant of the status of African Americans. He wrote in 1894: "When, finally, we consider the inferior position held by the negro race of the United States, who are in the closest contact with modern civilization, we must not forget that the old race-feeling of the inferiority of the colored is as potent as ever and is a formidable obstacle to its advance and progress, not withstanding that schools and universities are open to them. We might rather wonder how much has been accomplished in a short period against heavy odds. It is hardly possible to say what would become of the negro if he were able to live with the whites on absolutely equal terms."[51]

By 1909 he thought anthropology had demonstrated "that the impression which we gain from the failure of the American Negro to manifest himself in any of these directions [industry and art] is due, not to native inability, but to the degrading conditions under which he has been placed for generations."[52] In 1911 he argued that the purported "traits of the American negro are adequately explained on the basis of his history and

social status. . . . The tearing-away from the African soil and the consequent complete loss of the old standards of life, which were replaced by the
dependency of slavery and by all it entailed, followed by a period of disorganization and by a severe economic struggle against heavy odds, are sufficient to explain the inferiority of the status of the race, without falling back
upon the theory of hereditary inferiority."[53]

In 1915 Boas declared that white racism was far more insidious than
anti-Semitism in the United States: "The Negro of our times carries even
more heavily the burden of his racial descent than did the Jew of an earlier
period; and the intellectual and moral qualities required to insure success
to the Negro are infinitely greater than those demanded from the white,
and will be greater, the stricter the segregation of the Negro community."
Boas believed white prejudice served an important practical function. He
drew an analogy between prejudice and "the old instinct and fear of the
connubium of patricians and plebeians, of the European nobility and
common people, or of the castes of India." These "emotions and reasoning," he suggested, related "particularly to the necessity of maintaining a
distinct social status in order to avoid race-mixture." Sociologists, who
were the leading authorities on the issue of prejudice, assumed that it was
either "instinctive" or in "the mores," and that whites especially opposed
racial intermixture because they identified racial solidarity with cultural
solidarity. Although Boas argued that white prejudice was "not a physiological dislike"—as proved by the existence of a large mulatto
population—it was nevertheless, as the sociologists had argued, "an expression of social conditions that are so deeply ingrained . . . they assume
a strong emotional value." He concluded that although laws might "retard
the influx of white blood considerably, they cannot hinder the gradual
progress of intermixture."[54]

In the 1890s leading American anthropologists such as Daniel Garrison
Brinton, John Wesley Powell, and Frederic Ward Putnam were convinced
that there was a pattern of cultural evolution, and they posited that cultures
evolved through the progressive stages of savagery, barbarism, and civilization. In assuming that their civilization was the most progressive, the
major American anthropologists were white supremacists. Typical of the
Victorian mind-set in regard to the ability of blacks to achieve civilization
were Brinton's comments in 1890 in *Races and Peoples*:

> The low intellectual position of the Austrafrican [black] race is re-
> vealed by the facts that in no part of the [African] continent did its
> members devise the erection of walls of stone; that they domesticated
> no animal, and developed no important food-plant; that their religions

never rose above fetishism, their governments above despotism, their marriage relations above polygamy. It is true that many of them practice agriculture and the pastoral life, but it is significant that the plants which they especially cultivate, the "durra" or sorghum, millet, rice, yams, manioc, and tobacco, were introduced from Asia, Europe or America. The cattle and sheep are descended from the ancient stocks domesticated by the Egyptians, and differ from those represented on the early monuments of Assyria and India. The brick-built cities of the Sudan were constructed under Arab influence, and the ruins of stone towers and walls in the gold-bearing districts of South Africa show clear traces of Semitic workmanship.[55]

According to Brinton, Africans were unable to achieve the stage of civilization, primarily because of their racially limited intellectual capabilities. A former medical doctor who had been appointed professor of linguistics and folklore at the University of Pennsylvania in 1886, Brinton was typical of northern white supremacists in anthropology who thought the indigenous peoples of Africa were intellectually inferior to other races. "The powerful monarchies which at times have been erected in that continent over the dead bodies of myriads of victims," he wrote in *The Basis of Social Relations*, a posthumous work published in 1902, "have lasted but a generation or two. The natural limitations of the racial mind prevented it."[56]

Boas rose to challenge Brinton in 1894. Convinced that the Arabs "were the carriers of civilization" to the blacks of the Sudan, he wrote:

> Principally between the second half of the eighth century and the eleventh century of our era, the Soudan was invaded by Hamitic tribes and Mohammedanism was spreading rapidly through the Sahara and the Western Soudan. We see that, since that time, large empires were formed and disappeared again in struggles with neighboring states and that a relatively high degree of culture has been attained. The invaders intermarried with the natives, and the mixed races, some of which are almost purely negro, have risen high above the level of other African negroes. The history of Bornu is perhaps one of the best examples of this kind.[57]

Although Boas's emphasis on African empires was an important corrective of views prevailing in American anthropology, his perspective was limited by the suggestion that the Hamites were for the most part responsible for whatever heights the civilizations in the Sudan attained before the sixteenth century. At this point Boas was a diffusionist. Later, however, he would come to appreciate the genius of the indigenous peoples especially of West Africa, and his interpretation of African history led him to conclude

that the achievements of Africans in their indigenous environment represented the true capacity of the black race.

Boas began to disseminate these views as early as 1904, after he had
inspected African material culture as found in European museums of the
early 1900s. On the basis of what he had seen there, he wrote an article for
the *Ethical Record* titled, "What the Negro Has Done in Africa." Writing
with practically no knowledge of African American history, Boas argued
that it was unfair "to form a judgment of the whole [black] race by con-
sidering what it has done under trying conditions." Rather than gauge the
abilities of the black by the "work he accomplished as a slave" and "his advances since he obtained freedom, whites ought rather to look at the negro
in his own home, and see what advances in culture he has made there."
Boas pointed out that blacks in Africa had contributed "more than any
other [race] to the early development of the iron industry." Furthermore,
he asserted, they had worked out "strict methods of legal procedure," built
up local trade, organized their communities, assimilated foreign cultures,
and established powerful states in the Sudan. "The achievements of the
negro in Africa, therefore," he concluded, "justify us in maintaining that
the race is capable of social and political achievements; that it will produce
here, as it has done in Africa, its great men; and that it will contribute its
part to the welfare of the community."[58]

Hoping to arouse interest in the situation of African Americans, Boas
proposed in a 1906 letter to Felix Adler the founding of an "African
Museum" to present to the public "the best products of African civilization."[59] He sketched out his rationale for founding such a museum in a
proposal for funds which he sent to the businessman-philanthropist
Andrew Carnegie, on November 30, 1906: "It seems unfair to judge the
Negro by what he [has] come to be in America . . . [when] the evidence of
cultural achievement of the Negro in Africa suggests that his inventiveness,
power of political organization, and steadiness of purpose, equal or excel
those of other races of similar stages of culture."[60]

Writing to the philanthropist George A. Plimpton on May 10, 1907,
Boas also indicated that he wanted to bring his own data before the public:

> Even well-informed people assume that several very fundamental
> points have been established by scientific inquiry, particularly a less
> degree of mental capacity in the negro, a short period of mental
> development in the child, and a less degree of vitality. My investiga-
> tions . . . show very clearly that nothing has ever been established
> either one way or the other, and that all the material that we have so far
> at our disposal, when viewed without bias, merely shows trifling differ-
> ences between the two races . . . [which are] small as compared to the

differences between the less favorably organized whites and the more favorably organized whites in any of the European peoples; or, if I may express it in another way, that if we have a hundred negroes and a hundred whites, we can always match eighty and more of all the individuals, while there may perhaps be twenty negroes who are different from the whites, not necessarily inferior to them, and twenty whites who are different from the negroes, not necessarily superior to them.

Furthermore, I think every effort should be made to dispel the popular delusion that shiftlessness and the tendency to sexual depravity are in any way racial characteristics of the negro . . . by bringing out the data that are known in relation to the negro as he exists in Africa, uninfluenced by the whites. The political organizations of negro states, the great number of strong individualities, of powerful chiefs, and the high artistic development of native industries, afford ample proof of this.[61]

In the presence of African Americans, Boas became even more assertive. On October 11, 1905, W.E.B. Du Bois invited Boas to come to Atlanta University the following May to speak on the "African physique." On October 21, Boas told his colleague Edward T. Devine that he "should like very much to do a paper on the subject Du Bois suggested; but I think an opportunity of this kind should be used to present really new evidence and new points of view which would be helpful in gaining a new approach to our practical problem."[62]

The full implications of Boas's interpretation of the African past for African Americans were evident in the commencement address he delivered at Atlanta University on May 30, 1906. He began by suggesting that African Americans who had imbibed the idea of self-criticism (promulgated by Booker T. Washington and others) should certainly devote themselves to racial uplift: "If you did accept the view that the present weakness of the American Negro, his uncontrolled emotions, his lack of energy, are racially inherent, your work would still be a notable one. You, the more fortunate members of your race would give your life to a great charitable work, to support the unsteady gait of your weak brother who is too feeble to walk by himself." Boas did not want educated blacks to become pragmatic racial uplifters, however; rather, he had a vision of them as "happy idealists" who, despite a "dim future," would seek fulfillment through responsibility. These blacks, the distinguished anthropologist believed, had "the full right to view" their "labor in an entirely different light." Drawing on African history, he declared that "at a time when the European was still satisfied with rude stone tools, the African had invented or adopted the art of smelting iron." After pointing to several "arts of life" for which black Africans were responsible, Boas concluded that educated African Americans should be inspired to high achievements, and he spoke in optimistic tones about the future: "If, therefore, it is claimed that your race is doomed to economic inferiority, you may confidently look to the home of your ancestors and say, that you have set out to recover for the colored people the strength that was their own before they set foot on the shores of this continent. You may say that you go to work with bright hopes, and that you will not be discouraged by the slowness of your progress; for you have to recover not only what has been lost in transplanting the Negro race from its native soil to this continent, but you must reach higher levels than your ancestors had ever attained.[63]

Although as late as 1909 Boas still thought some contemporary stereotypes of African Americans were true, he evidently did not believe that West and Central Africans—the peoples from whom most African Americans were descended—conformed to those stereotypes. It is important to note where he thought the responsibility lay for the conditions of African Americans:

> The essential point that anthropology can contribute to the practical discussion of the adaptability of the Negro is a decision on the question of how far the undesirable traits that are at present undoubtedly found in our Negro population are due to racial traits, and how far they are due to social surroundings for which *we* are responsible. To this question anthropology can give the decided answer that the traits of the African culture as observed in the aboriginal home of the Negro are those of a healthy primitive people with a considerable degree of personal initiative, with a talent for organization.[64]

Boas attacked three weaknesses in the argument of the proponents of black inferiority. First, the stereotypes suggesting that West Africans were innately indolent and unable to defer gratification were fallacious. Describing the industrial life in the typical West African village, he wrote:

> Village life is replete with activity. The extensive gardens of the village must be tilled; the loom is busy; in the hands of the women plastic clay is made into useful pottery ware; the woodcarver makes dishes and other articles for the home and adorns them with fanciful carvings; the blacksmith's bellows are busy and his hammer may be heard. The produce of the field and the work of the artisan are packed up and carried to the market which is held at regular intervals, and where distant tribes may meet to exchange their commodities.[65]

Second, against the stereotype of blacks as lacking men of strong willpower, Boas presented evidence suggesting that some African leaders had succeeded in organizing large "political and military empires that have endured for many generations." Third, Boas undermined the myth that only northern and western European peoples had made significant historical achievements; he did so by arguing the likelihood that "the art of making iron implements may have been first invented on the African continent by the Negro race." Their industrial and artistic works and political achievements led Boas to declare unequivocally that "the impression which we gain from the failure of the American Negro to manifest himself in any of these directions is due, not to native inability, but to the degrading condition under which he has been placed for generations."[66]

By emphasizing the glories of the African past, Boas was trying to build a special tradition for African Americans. He was trying, he wrote Starr Murphy on November 23, 1906, to combat "a strong feeling of despondency among the best classes of the Negro, due to the economic, mental, and moral inferiority of the race in America." When he spoke to southern African Americans of "their parental race in their native surroundings," Boas added, he had noticed that the "facts were a complete revelation to them."[67]

As he wrote later, blacks retained few if any vestiges of their African heritage in North America, "where loss of continuity of development and inferior social position have made a deep impression on the race that will be slow to disappear."[68]

Also indicative of Boas's belief that African Americans needed a stronger cultural identity was his support of Carter G. Woodson, who asked him on March 17, 1920, to assist in "directing attention to the Negro as a constructive element in this country that the race by scientific research, rather than by agitation and politics, obtain a hearing at the bar of public opinion." Woodson proposed to establish a journal, and Boas—who would later serve on the publication's executive council—replied on March 29, 1920: "I consider your undertaking, the Journal of Negro History, a very valuable one. . . . I do hope that you will be able to continue its publication which must be of considerable help in developing a sane and scientific point of view in regard to the whole negro question."[69] Boas was no cultural pluralist however; he simply believed that once the historical facts were known in reference to blacks, racial antagonism would diminish, and the whole attitude of the white population "in regard to the Negro might be materially modified"—thereby facilitating the assimilation process.[70] The myth of African inferiority, however, sustained itself past the first decade of the twentieth century in the discipline of anthropology, despite the political domination of Boas, who had undermined the basis of that myth in the articles he published between 1904 and 1909.

It lingered in other disciplines as well. In sociology, Jerome Dowd, a North Carolinian who studied briefly at the University of Chicago, described the diverse West African peoples in his two-volume work *The Negro Races* and concluded that their societies were "abnormal or retrogressive." He based his claim on the argument of physical anthropologists who believed the West African's brain was "so constituted that its sensorimotor activities predominate over his idio-motor activities; i.e., his passions and natural impulses are exceptionally potent and his inhibiting power exceptionally feeble." The infiltration of the theme of African barbarism into the *American Journal of Sociology* and the *Annals of the American Academy of Political and Social Science* was immediate. Yet though the idea of the "abnormal and retrogressive" nature of the African has been extremely potent, sustaining itself in the popular mind to this day, the myth of African inferiority in the discipline of sociology began to be eclipsed with the publication of Ellsworth Faris's "The Mental Capacity of Savages" in the *American Journal of Sociology* in 1918—and, indeed, Faris acknowledged his debt to Boas.[71]

In the discipline of history the myth of African inferiority was boldly sketched out by Joseph A. Tillinghast, a descendant of an old Rhode Island family and the son of a South Carolina slaveholder. Tillinghast stated emphatically in *The Negro in Africa and America* (1902) that West Africans had "no great industrial system, no science, and art" primarily because they were incapable of exercising "foresight" and inhibiting their "sexual proclivities."[72] Tillinghast's and Dowd's myth was potent; after 1915 it surfaced in the influential works of Ulrich B. Phillips. For example, in his influential *American Negro Slavery* (1918) Phillips described the ancestors of African Americans:

> The inhabitants of Guinea, and of the coast lands especially, have survived by retreating and adapting themselves to conditions in which no others wished to dwell. The requirements of adaptation were peculiar. To live where nature supplies Turkish baths without the asking necessitates relaxation. But since undue physical indolence would unfit people for resistance to parasites and hostile neighbors, the languid would perish. Relaxation of mind, however, brought no penalties. The climate in fact not only discourages but prohibits mental effort of severe or sustained character, and the negroes have submitted to that prohibition as to many others, through countless generations, with excellent grace.[73]

Like Tillinghast and Dowd, Phillips—a native of Georgia who taught at both the University of Wisconsin and Yale—was a southerner intent on creating in effect a myth of the antebellum South to rationalize the blatant forms of racism that characterized the South during the Progressive era. But as Eugene D. Genovese has correctly pointed out, Phillips's racism "could not have stood critical examination even in his day."[74]

I have emphasized Boas's thought on Africa and the reaction to it not only because he was a white man in the elite who cultivated cosmopolitan values but also because he had a direct impact on the image of Africa in the thought of W.E.B. Du Bois, Booker T. Washington, George W. Ellis, Monroe N. Work, and Carter G. Woodson. Commenting on Boas's 1906 commencement address in Atlanta and its importance to his own later development as one of the leading American students of Africa, Du Bois wrote in 1939:

> I remember my own sudden awakening from the paralysis of this judgment [that African Americans had no history] taught me in high school and in two of the world's greatest universities. Franz Boas came to Atlanta University where I was teaching history in 1906 and said to a graduating class: "You need not be ashamed of your African past"; and then he recounted the history of the black kingdoms south of the Sahara for a thousand years. I was too astonished to speak. All of this I had never heard and I came then and afterwards to realize how silence and neglect of science can let truth utterly disappear or even be consciously distorted. [75]

Boas's conception of African history also influenced neo-abolitionists such as Horace Bumstead, the white president of predominantly black Atlanta University. Citing Franz Boas in 1908, Bumstead wrote: "Let us rid our minds of the picture of the Negro as he is burlesqued in the comic papers and on the cover of the shoe-blacking-box . . . and get a higher conception of him. . . . [White people are] still too much under the sway of antiquated teaching in regard to the Negro in Africa. From childhood we have been fed with stories of the ignorant and lazy savages. . . . But more recent investigations are presenting a very different picture."[76]

Even more important, Boas influenced a younger generation of African Americans. Willis Huggins, a student at Columbia University's Teachers College, was thankful for his insights into the African past. On October 16, 1911, with an enthusiasm that ignored Boas's ambivalences, Huggins wrote to him:

> Having read and studied your article in the Sunday Times of September 24th upon the ancient civilization of Nature [sic] African Races and your more recent article of October first upon "Human Types," I take great pleasure in expressing to you my appreciation of such timely information you gave out concerning the initiative in self-government that the race to which I belong has shown. I regard your articles, not merely as a retort of refutation of views recently given out by a distinguished Georgian, but almost solely as the natural procedure from a

friend of facts that none but an unbiased scientist and seeker after facts, could collect. I took pleasure in reading yours of Sept. 24th to a gathering of young colored men in the local branch of the Colored Y.M.C.A. and to a man who voiced appreciation of your careful research and signal fairplay. On behalf of those young men and also that great horde of young negro men and women who have lined themselves up upon this side of law and order in this country I do most ardently thank you. That army of Negro youth who are daily struggling for education so as to be a greater service to his people have much to be thankful for in the products of your research. [77]

Despite his adulation of young African Americans such as Willis Huggins, the thought of Franz Boas on blacks remained paradoxical as late as 1915. He was still torn between his commitment to physical anthropological assumptions, which suggested that the races were not equal, and his commitment to cultural anthropology, which suggested that white prejudice was an obvious obstacle to black progress. His study of the material culture and history of the West African ancestors of African Americans was still in dynamic equilibrium with his assumption of black physical inferiority. Boas's egalitarian instincts would eventually win out, however, as the relentless social-structural changes that had brought the "social problems" of blacks into visibility after 1900 were exacerbated by the migration of more blacks to New York City during World War I. Furthermore, Boas—whose own ethnic group was being subjected to abuse by immigration restrictionists, businessmen like Henry Ford, proponents of 100 percent Americanism, and Ku Klux Klan—was especially disturbed by the upsurge of both nativist and racial ideologies and practices that gained momentum during the 1920s.[78]

In "The Problem of the American Negro," published in the *Yale Quarterly Review* in 1921 (from which his "men of high genius" hypothesis was conspicuously absent), Boas attacked racists by criticizing their interpretations of anthropometric data. After reviewing the findings of physical anthropologists, he did not draw invidious distinctions between blacks and whites; willingly admitting that "on the average, the brain of the negro is slightly smaller than the brain of the European," he nevertheless surmised, "The response on the part of brains of different structure and size to the demands of life may be very much the same."[79]

Furthermore, Boas was critical of some psychological experiments. Early in his career he had believed that experimental psychology would provide definitive insights into racial mental differences; twenty-seven years later he recognized that many investigations into the mental abilities of black and white children were biased. Boas wrote: "I am not convinced that the results that have been obtained are significant in regard to racial ability as a whole. The variability of the results is also very marked and there is an overlapping of racial traits." He was intent on pushing the liberal environmentalist argument as far as possible. Responding to a study by M.R. Trabue which was based on the army's culturally biased Alpha and Beta tests, Boas argued that northern blacks were not inherently superior to southern blacks, nor was it true that only "the gifted Southern negroes emigrated."[80] In a lucid passage he argued that prejudice adversely affected test results:

> In the absence of sound proof this [inherent intellectual] superiority may just as well be explained by the assumption that Northern negroes are exposed to a wider range of experience than Southern negroes. Anyone who knows the abject fear of the Southern negroes who are put under the control of an unknown white officer in foreign surroundings, anyone who knows the limitations of early childhood and general upbringing of negroes in the South, will accept these findings, but will decline to accept them as a convincing proof of the hereditary inferiority of the negro race.[81]

To prove that cultural factors were more significant than heredity to an understanding of the plight of African Americans, Boas again turned to a discussion of African achievements to demonstrate that the traits of African Americans were not racial traits. He believed that Africans were industrially more advanced than other primitive people and that their "native arts" such as weaving, carving, pottery, blacksmithing, metalcasting, and glassblowing were "excellent." Furthermore, the political organization of black Africans resembled the political organization in medieval Europe; African states in the Sudan, the Congo, and South Africa had "negro rulers whose genius for organization has enabled them to establish flourishing empires."[82] (Boas did not attempt to speak on whether or not the "negro rulers" could enter his realm of "men of high genius," however.)

Another article that demonstrated Boas's maturing thought was "What Is Race?" which appeared in *The Nation* in 1925 and in which he sought to delimit the boundaries of the Nature-versus-Nurture controversy. He mentioned blacks only once, yet the implications for the "Negro problem" were clear. Unlike his pre-1920 writings, this article argued that it was wrongheaded to try to "judge" an individual "by the size of his brain" or by his physiological or mental functions, mainly because those forms and functions "vary enormously in each race, and many features that are found in one race are also found belonging to other races." Indeed, it was "impossible to speak of hereditary racial characteristics because the traits characterizing any individual occur in a number of human races." Obvious differences in the appearance and behavior of certain "social groups" did not "imply that these characteristics are hereditarily determined"; rather, "racial strains, when subject to the same social environment, develop the same functional tendencies." As for the controversial issue of mental differences, Boas pointed out correctly that the "occurrence of hereditary mental traits that belong to a particular race has never been proved"; thus it was safe to infer that the "behavior of an individual is therefore not determined by his racial affiliations, but by the character of his ancestry and his cultural environment." One could "judge the mental characteristics of families and individuals, but not of races."[83]

By 1928, when *Anthropology and Modern Life* was published, Boas was appalled at how much literature was "based on the assumption that each race has its own mental character determining its cultural or social behavior." He stated unequivocally that the concept of racial types was "based on subjective experience"; there were "no pure races." Yet it would be an overstatement to assert that Boas had completely rid himself of racist anthropological assumptions. He still argued that "the distribution of individuals and of family lines in the various races differs. When we select among the Europeans a group with large brains, their frequency will be relatively high, while among the Negroes the frequency of occurrence of the corresponding group will be low. If, for instance, there are 50 percent of a European population who have a brain weight of more than, let us say, 1,500 grams, there may be only 20 percent of Negroes of the same class. Therefore, 30 percent of the large-brained Europeans cannot be matched by any corresponding group of Negroes." Boas considered the practice of comparing the brain sizes of races justifiable as long as "we avoid an application of our results to individuals": "It is not possible," he asserted firmly, "to identify an individual as a Negro or White according to the size and form of the brain, but serially the Negro brain is less extremely human than that of the White."[84]

A captive of nineteenth-century physical anthropology, Boas never quite escaped. As late as 1938 his "men of high genius" hypothesis reappeared in the highly revised edition of *The Mind of Primitive Man*. And although the social-structural changes of his time would have emancipatory implications for blacks after World War II, racism triumphed in anthropology and sociology for another decade and a half. Its persistence in disciplines dedicated to determining the laws of human nature give credence to Fredrickson's statement that "history in general does not . . . provide much basis for the notion that passionately held fallacies are destined to collapse because they are in conflict with empirical reality."[85]

Boas's thought on African Americans reflected both the strengths and weaknesses of the "American conscience" during the years before 1945. In seeking to reform white America's attitudes by developing the science of culture, Boas provided that conscience with a "scientific" antiracist foundation. The United States would only gradually accommodate an antiracist critique. African Americans would have to await the Second Reconstruction.

2

Boas and the African American Intelligentsia

Marshall Hyatt argued in 1990 that Franz Uri Boas throughout his long career used blacks as a "camouflage . . . for attacking all forms of prejudice."[1] In other words, Hyatt saw Boas's indictment of antiblack racism as part of his desire to protect his own ethnic group. Yet Boas's correspondence with leading African American intellectuals such as Booker T. Washington, W.E.B. Du Bois, Carter G. Woodson, Alain L. Locke, George E. Haynes, Abram Harris, Charles S. Johnson, Monroe N. Work, Charles H. Thompson, and Zora Neale Hurston reveals that he not only displayed an astonishing degree of real empathy with the plight of African American intellectuals and the black masses but also performed such practical functions as assisting them in obtaining jobs and foundation support, fighting for academic freedom, and nurturing studies of African American history and life in the social sciences. As a result of his long-term support of African Americans and their causes, some members of the intelligentsia, in turn, were supportive of him when the Nazis' propaganda and atrocities were revealed to the general public in the late 1930s.

Boas's influence on the African American intelligentsia, whose nineteenth-century heritage was a primary force in motivating them to link race to traits of character, ability, and behavior, was of monumental significance. Thanks to him, their acceptance of the (relatively benign) inherited doctrine that each race had an innate social character withered away by the 1930s.

For Du Bois, as well as for Kelly Miller and Monroe N. Work, physical anthropology held the key to the nature of racial differences. All three scholars felt compelled to recontextualize the dominant discourse on race in physical anthropology, which was directed by the pronouncements of Frederick L. Hoffman in his 1896 book *Race Traits and Tendencies of the American Negro*. Hoffman, a German-born employee of the Prudential Insurance Company, claimed to be "free from personal bias which might have made an impartial treatment of the subject difficult."[2] Nevertheless, the conclusion of his work was an expression of the rampant Darwinism that predicted the impending extinction of African Americans. It was Hoffman's argument that African Americans were deteriorating physically and morally, and doing so because of their "race traits and tendencies" rather than because of the adverse conditions to which they had been subjected; it was "not in the conditions of life but in race and heredity that we find the explanation." Persons of mixed ancestry were, according to Hoffman, subject to the same deterioration—primarily because "the mixture of the African with the white race has shown to have seriously affected the longevity of the former and left as a heritage to future generations the poison of scrofula, tuberculosis and most of all, of syphillis."[3]

In a thirty-three page review (the first publication of the American Negro Academy) Kelly Miller took Hoffman to task. Miller, professor of mathematics at Howard University since 1890, had studied mathematics, physics, and astronomy under Simon Newcomb at the Naval Observatory and had all the skills needed to expose Hoffman's fallacies. He demonstrated that "leaving immigration out of account, the increase in the Negro population is greater than that of the white race." "How can these two facts," Miller asked, "be accounted for except it be on the basis of a higher birthrate for the blacks?"[4] In order to reveal Hoffman's error in attributing to "race traits" the morbidity and mortality of African Americans from certain diseases, Miller compared them with working-class whites in Germany and showed that the "high death rate of the American Negro did not exceed that of the white race in other parts of the civilized globe." Miller asked: "If race traits are playing such havoc with the Negroes in America, what direful agent of death . . . is at work in the cities of [Hoffman's] own fatherland?"[5]

Hoffman, relying on the work of B.A. Gould and other examining surgeons during the Civil War, held that the admixture of blacks and whites "has contributed more than anything else to the excessive and increasing rate of mortality from the most fatal disease, as well as to its consequent social efficiency and diminishing power as a force in American national life." To Hoffman's argument that the mulatto is physically inferior to both parent races, Miller responded: "The last word of science has not been uttered on this questions. . . . The Freedmen's Hospital at Washington and similar institutions elsewhere, by prosecuting accurate and scientific methods of inquiry can throw much light upon this subject." As to moral inferiority in the mulatto, which Hoffman based on statistics from the eleventh census, Miller stated: "Supposing the uniform methods of race-tests were used throughout the census inquiry, this would show that while the mixed Negroes constitute only 16 per cent of the total Negro population, they furnished 30 per cent of the penitentiary convicts. But these figures cannot be relied upon since the census bureau acknowledges that it has no definite method of determining the different shades of color and grades of mixture among Negroes." Finally, there was the mulatto's alleged intellectual superiority to blacks (but inferiority to whites); Hoffman based this proposition on the contention that most African Americans who had attained distinction were of mixed blood. Miller agreed but thought the cause was that the "initial advantage of the mixed over the pure Negroes was considerable. Feelings of blood ties prompted many a slaveholder to deal kindly by his slave descendants, and often to liberate them and give them a start in the race of life." And even so, there were outstanding African Americans of the "purer type," such as Phillis Wheatley, Benjamin Bannaker, Ira Aldridge, Blind Tom, Edward W. Blyden, and Paul Dunbar. Quoting Ripley, Miller pointed out that Hoffman's evidence, which was based on facial angle, capacity of the cranium, and the cephalic index, "afford[s] no certain criterion of the power of susceptibility to culture."[6]

To Hoffman's further assertion that religion and education could not uplift African Americans because it was "not on the conditions of life but in race and heredity" that the "Negro Problem" lay, Miller wrote: "The philanthropists [who fund black religious and educational institutions] have made no mistake. They have proceeded on the supposition that the Negro has faculty and power for power with the rest of his fellow men, and that his special needs grow out of his peculiar condition. Any alteration of this policy would violate the dictates both of science and humanity." In Miller's opinion, Hoffman had based his conclusion on "*a priori* considerations," and his "facts have been collected in order to justify it. . . . It is a condition and not a theory that confronts [the African American]."[7]

During this same period W.E.B. Du Bois was attempting to discredit the view that African Americans composed a homogeneous group whose members (except the mulattoes) should be treated alike. Born in 1868 into a poor, female-headed household in Great Barrington, Massachussetts, Du Bois—as his biographer David Levering Lewis notes astutely—thought "the promise for salvation would lie in the social sciences, not the Bible." Both at Harvard University and during a sojourn in Germany (where the lack of funding prevented him from receiving a prestigious German doctorate), Du Bois thought the pursuit of social scientific truths would be the path to the creation of a colorblind, egalitarian society in the United States. Yet his assimilationist impulses were counterbalanced by his embrace of Hegel's philosophy, from which "he borrowed more or less intact notions of distinct, hierarchical racial attributes."[8] Alexander Crummell, the leading African American intellectual, also influenced significantly his belief in racial attributes. This tension can be seen throughout Du Bois's writings and life before 1919; he was often caught between attempting to initiate and strengthen black institutions and to fight internecine battles with white assimilationists and, at the same time, denouncing Jim Crow.

While Boas, on the basis of his anthropometric measurements and analysis of the African background of African Americans, was issuing the prescriptive statement that individual merit, not race, should determine a person's position in the American social order, Du Bois was uncovering empirical evidence and offering explanations for the stratification that existed among African Americans in the 1890s. Indeed, the idea of an African American class structure had its origins in the turn-of-the-century scholarship of Du Bois and has persisted for almost a century as a key analytical concept in social scientific discussion of race relations in the United States. At present, it raises important questions about the relative significance of "race" and "class" as determinants of the status of African Americans, and it is central to the arguments of such distinguished current scholars as Alphonso Pinkney, Thomas Sowell, and William J. Wilson.

Du Bois's concept of an African American class structure grew out of his attempt to rebut the Darwinian prediction of the impending extinction of African Americans as developed in Hoffman's *Race Traits*. To Du Bois it was apparent that Hoffman did not have the insight to offer a "proper interpretation of apparently contradictory social facts. . . . If, for instance, we find among American Negroes today, at the very same time, increasing intelligence and increasing crime, increasing wealth and disproportionate poverty, increasing religious and moral activity and high rate of illegitimacy in births, we can no more fasten upon the bad as typifying the general tendancy than we can upon the good." Arguing emphatically against Hoffman's assumption that such contradictory facts pertained to "the race" rather than to the class structure that had developed since emancipation, Du Bois believed that the extent of an African American's progress or retrogression was determined by the individual's rank within the black class structure. He was certain that white prejudice was an obstacle to black progress because it kept more blacks in the lower class. Like the white progressives, he assumed that lower-class people were less intelligent and more prone to immoral activity.

Du Bois, whose orientation was a product both of his inferior status as an African American in an Anglo-American-dominated society and of his academic training in the United States and Germany, anticipated the work of Robert E. Park and W. Lloyd Warner in the first three decades of the twentieth century. In his 1899 book, *The Philadelphia Negro*, Du Bois gathered empirical data suggesting that class differentiation already existed in black America: "Wide variations in antecedents, wealth, intelligence and general efficiency have already been differentiated with[in] this [African

American] group." But even as he emphasized the differentiation in Philadelphia's major black community, he amassed ample evidence that the attitudes and behavior of the white population "limited and circumscribed"
the opportunities of even "the better classes" of African Americans.[9] Thus,
for Du Bois, despite the class structure among African Americans, "race"
was the most salient variable in American race relations.

For members of the African American educated elite, the implications of Boas's assessments of the cranial cavities of blacks and whites
were revolutionary. For an intellectual such as the Harvard-educated
W.E.B. Du Bois, Boas's analysis of anthropometric measurements of cranial
cavities was truly subversive. Du Bois was cognizant of the centrality of
physical anthropology as a buttress to the dominant discourse of race in
science; as early as 1898, in "The Study of the Negro Problems," he stated
that "anthropological measurement" was one of four "practical divisions"
for "the study of the Negro as a social group" and included "a scientific
study of the Negro body. The most obvious peculiarity of the Negro—a
peculiarity which is a large element in many problems affecting him—is his
physical unlikeness to the people with whom he has been brought into contact. This difference is so striking that it has become the basis of a mass of
theory, assumption and suggestion which is deep-rooted and yet rests on
the flimsiest basis of scientific fact. That there are differences between the
white and black races is certain, but just what those differences are is
known to none with an approach to accuracy."[10]

Du Bois initiated a relationship with Franz Boas in 1905, a friendship
that lasted for more than three decades. On October 11 of that year he
wrote to inform Boas that Atlanta University was planning to conduct a
study of the Negro physique and asked Boas's help in identifying the best
and latest works bearing on the anthropology of the blacks—particularly
their physical measurements, health, and so on. Du Bois indicated that the
Atlanta study would be a "great opportunity . . . for physical measurement
of the Negro," provided Columbia University would fund the project.[11] In
his reply on October 14, Boas indicated that he could not refer Du Bois "to
anything that is particularly good on the physical anthropology of the
Negro" but that he would query Columbia about the possibility of funding
a study of the physical anthropology of blacks.[12] He did not accept Du
Bois's invitation to attend the Atlanta University conference on May 29,
1906, but did deliver the university's commencement address on May 31,
speaking to an audience that included black working people, preachers, and
professionals on the African background of African Americans rather than
on their anthropometric measurement.

In *The Health and Physique of the Negro American*, which was based on
the anthropometric measurements of more than 1,000 students at Atlanta

University, Du Bois in 1906 quoted a memorandum by Monroe N. Work, who was teaching at Savannah State that year; Work took to task the conclusion of scholars such as Robert B. Bean that the brain of the African American was smaller than that of the Euro-American. Work, the son of former slaves, was born in Iredell County, North Carolina, in 1866. He was raised in Cairo, Illinois, and rural Kansas. Like many men who formed the ranks of the early sociologists, he first embarked on a ministerial career, joining the African Methodist Episcopal Church. Recalling his career from 1897 until 1903, Work related that he was studying at Chicago Theological Seminary on the city's west side when Graham Taylor, who taught what was called "Christian Sociology," became interested in a paper that Work had completed on black crime in Chicago. When Work changed his career aspiration from the ministry to sociology in 1898 and entered the University of Chicago to study under William I. Thomas, he took that paper with him. With some revisions, it was published in the *American Journal of Sociology* in 1900, the first article by an African American to appear in that journal.[13] After receiving his Master of Arts degree from the University of Chicago, Work accepted a position at Georgia State Industrial College in Savannah in order to be near W.E.B. Du Bois. Work considered himself, Du Bois, Richard R. Wright Jr., and Kelly Miller "the four [Negro] originals" in the newly formed discipline of sociology and was confident that Du Bois, through his pioneering work in Atlanta, held the key to a truly meaningful uplift of blacks. So closely was Work allied to Du Bois that he even joined the short-lived Niagara movement, a series of conferences in which prominent African American leaders protested the erosion of their civil rights during "the nadir."[14]

Although his memorandum made no reference to Boas (who had refuted Bean's argument that same year), Work concluded:

> The best evidence seems to indicate that the organization and, therefore, the details of the structure of the central nervous system are continually being modified through life. That is, changes are constantly occurring. These changes, which are many and varied, are caused by age, occupation, nutrition, disease, etc. This fact of constant change makes it very doubtful whether any uniformity in the finer details of structure will be found in white brains, particularly if they are brains of different sizes from persons of different ages, statures, etc., and the cause of death not being the same. These facts, in connection with the well established fact that those characters which are said to be distinctive of particular races are found with more or less frequency in other races, seem to indicate that what has been described as being peculiar in the size, shape, and anatomy of the Negro brain is not true of all Negro brains. These same peculiarities can no doubt be found in

many white brains and probably have no special connection with the
mental capacity of either race.[15]

Du Bois indeed understood the implications of Work's and Boas's assessment of anthropometric measurement for the myth of African Americans
as a homogeneous group. Speaking to the National Negro Conference
(which preceded the initial organization of the NAACP in 1909), he asserted that the conference address of Boas's disciple Livingston Ferrand
"left no doubt in the minds of listeners that the whole argument by which
Negroes were pronounced absolutely and inevitably inferior to whites was
utterly without scientific basis."[16] Du Bois, nevertheless, was uncritical of
Boas's reservations about black equality.

Boas's position influenced the thought even of moderate conservatives, such as Booker T. Washington, who were locked in a severe struggle
against the forces of racism and reaction in the South. This argument is
perhaps best illustrated by the correspondence between Washington
and T.E. Taylor, a representative of the sixty-seventh district in the Iowa
state legislature. Taylor wrote Washington on September 5, 1915, concerning an assertion by James K. Vardaman (Mississippi's governor,
1904–8), speaking in Independence, Iowa, "that the negro's skull hardens at
age of puberty and from that age on there is no mental development."
Taylor did not accept the theory and asked Washington, "What facts can
you give me on this point?"[17] In a long response, Washington referred
Taylor to the work of Franz Boas and William I. Thomas (a sociologist
whose work closely paralleled that of Boas) by Washington's private secretary, "For discussion of what the best scientists have to say concerning this
question I refer you to the recent volume of the Macmillan Company en-
titled 'The Mind of Primitive Man' by Professor Franz Boas of Columbia
University, who is, I understand, the leading authority on the question of
the mental ability of races. Another interesting discussion of this same subject is by Professor W.I. Thomas of the University of Chicago, in his book
on 'Sex and Society' in the chapter on 'Mind of Woman and the Lower
Races.' If your public library has the back numbers of the American Journal
of Sociology, you will find this same article by Professor Thomas published
therein sometime during the period 1906–1908."[18] Like Du Bois,
Washington and his Tuskegee colleagues interpreted Boas's position as an
attack on the crude racism that drew no distinctions between the relative
abilities of different blacks but considered all whites superior to all blacks.

For Alain LeRoy Locke, Boas's ideas were a point of departure. Born
in Philadelphia, Pennsylvania, in 1885, Locke trained in philosophy at
Harvard College from 1904 to 1907. As a Rhodes Scholar he then studied
Greek, philosophy, and *literae humaniores* at Oxford's Hertford College

between 1907 and 1910 and went on to the University of Berlin in 1910. Returning to Harvard in 1916, he completed his doctorate in philosophy over the next two years, at the same time serving as an assistant professor of English and instructor in philosophy and education at the Teachers College at Howard University in Washington D.C. One of the numerous strengths of this African American's lectures was their assault on the concept of biological race. For Locke, this concept—albeit still subject to clarification—was a "scientific fiction." Drawing on the work of Franz Uri Boas, he argued that biological race differences were negligible: "Because of differences [in] anthropological [factors,] points of comparison have now been reduced to such a narrow margin in each instance that the variation between individuals of the same race, and even the same nation, more than outspan the maximum variability between what are regarded as cognate races of mankind."[19] As a result, Locke thought it necessary to draw a distinction between "racial inequalities," which were to be explained "in terms of historical, economic, and social factors," and "racial differences," to be explained "in terms of anthropological and ethnological factors[,] and predicating another cause and effect [basis] for the relation between the two." Since race was a social or cultural phenomenon, Locke concluded that "any true history of race must be a sociological theory of race."[20]

The net effect of Boas's ideas, Locke noted, was to show that, "a really pure science of race is . . . undesirable, not so much because it is impossible, but because even though it were realized, it would be impracticable, particularly as contrasted with whatever current practical theories of race are prevailing in society. It could never successfully hope to compete with what men really believe human society to be." Locke concluded: "To the extent, therefore, that any man has race, he has inherited either a favorable or an unfavorable social heredity, which unfortunately is [typically] ascribed to factors which have not produced [it], factors which will in no way determine either the period of those inequalities or their eradication."[21]

Boas influenced not only participants in the academy but other members of the African American elite as well. George Washington Ellis, a historically significant but neglected figure, was a Chicago-based attorney and former diplomat. Since there is no biography of Ellis, and documents regarding his life before 1905 are scanty, we have only a bare outline of his accomplishments before he reached thirty years of age. We do know, however, that he was born to George Ellis and Amanda Jane Trace in Weston, Platte County, Missouri, in 1875.[22] He left his hometown after completing elementary school because it did not provide sufficient educational opportunities and went to Kansas City, Missouri. Although he found greater opportunities in that city, Ellis found that he was "under the pressure of prejudice" and migrated to Atchison, Kansas, where he completed high school in 1891.[23] He went on to law school at the University of Kansas that same year and was awarded the L.L.B. there in 1893. While pursuing his B.A. at Kansas, he practiced law in order to defray his expenses and was active in Republican state politics. Variously referred to as "the bright and brilliant attorney," "an eloquent colored orator," and "an able exponent of the currency question" in Kansas newspapers, Ellis was selected as one of the debaters in the McKinley Club and treasurer of his university class.[24] After taking his Bachelor of Arts in 1897, he migrated to New York City and took courses at the Gunton Institute of Economics and Sociology.

In 1899, as a result of his activities as a Republican speaker and his scores on a federal examination, Ellis was appointed to the Census Division of the Department of the Interior. While working in Washington, Ellis found time to take philosophy and psychology courses in the School of Pedagogy at Howard University and to participate in an investigation that resulted in a work compiled and edited by Andrew F. Hilyer titled *Colored Washington*. Furthermore, Ellis, described by one newspaper as "one of the most efficient and popular clerks in the Census Office," caught the attention of President Theodore Roosevelt and was appointed secretary of the United States legation in the Republic of Liberia.[25] During his tenure there from 1902 to 1910, his investigations and reports of the numerous and diverse tribes in the interior significantly shaped the State Department's policies toward Liberia. In addition, Ellis completed a significant ethnographic study that was very sympathetic to the Vai-speaking people of Liberia—the only sub-Saharan African group of this period who had developed an orthography—which, after some years of rejection, was published in 1914.

In the *Journal of Race Development* (to which he was a frequent contributor) Ellis concluded in 1915 that "ethnological science has been . . . an influential factor in creating, diffusing and crystallizing race prejudice in the social minds of whites." But the "new ethnology" written by Franz Boas and Alexander Chamberlain (a former student of Boas and the editor of the journal to which Ellis was contributing, in which Ellis believed the truth was being told concerning blacks and whites) asserted that "physical features, the cephalic angle, the texture of hair, the shape of the head, the color of the skin, the size or shape, or the size and weight of the brain, have *little or nothing* [emphasis added] to do with the capacity of mind or the moral quality of the soul; that like other race varieties, the Negro is a product of the complex and subtle forces of his milieu . . . acting upon him for centuries past; that there is no naturally superior and inferior race, and that no race has a monopoly on either beauty, intellect or culture."[26]

In short, the African American elite—which, like the participants in the dominant discourse—had conceived of "race" as a supraindividual organic entity and used such terms as racial "essence," racial "genius," racial "soul," and racial "message," became aware that Boas offered them by far the best deal they were going to get, and they took it. The African American elite, which was either more biologically assimilated or more acculturated than the black masses, accepted Boas's ideas uncritically—primarily because his argument seemed to suggest that caste barriers did not recognize color and class distinctions; they now had an argument for their acceptance on an individual basis. Thus, even though Boas's philosophy suggested that proportionally few of them could shape history, it did suggest that there was no reason a goodly number should be excluded from participating in society.

During the 1920s and 1930s, as several historians have noted, Boas and his students—most notably Margaret Mead, Melville J. Herskovits, and Otto Klineberg—were critical of the methodologies of such psychologists as George Oscar Ferguson, Carl C. Brigham, Joseph Peterson, and Lewis M. Peterson. These were the formulators of the army's Alpha and Beta "intelligence" tests, used to prove "scientifically" that the vast majority of African Americans were inferior to persons descended from northern and western Europeans.[27] And according to the historian Vincent P. Franklin, African American psychologists as well—Howard Hale Long, Horace Mann Bond, Herman Canady, Martin D. Jenkins, Joseph St. Clair Price, and Doxey Wilkerson—were skeptical of the claims of Euro-American intelligence testers and published refutations of white psychologists' conclusions between 1923 and 1936.[28]

It is interesting to note that some African American social scientists, in their effort to recontextualize the findings of scientific racists, sought the expertise and support of Franz Boas. On April 13, 1925, Charles S. Johnson—who was editor of the National Urban League's *Opportunity: Journal of Negro Life* and who would go on to establish himself as one of the country's leading authorities on race relations—wrote Boas concerning an article by Howard Hale Long of the Department of Research of the Washington, D.C., public schools. Long's thesis, Johnson wrote, "which seems to be extraordinarily well supported, questions seriously the validity of psychological comparisons of races based upon the current mental tests." Long had "measured and studied thousands of children of different races," and "his results seem to show that the mental age of white and colored children are not commensurable; that a mental age on the Binet scale for a colored child means more than the same mental age on the same scale for a white child; and that although a colored child might actually have a mental ability, equal to that of a white child, he would nevertheless have a lower mental age."[29] Boas responded on April 25, 1925, that he was "interested" in reading the paper and asked Johnson to forward him a copy of it.[30]

What became of Long's paper is unknown, but by 1928 Boas was working on a study of intelligence tests. Abram Harris, one of his former students who went on to establish himself as a leading economist, wrote Boas concerning a meeting he had had with Charles H. Thompson, professor of education at Howard University, who had received his doctorate in educational psychology at the University of Chicago. Thompson was interested, "in making an analysis of cultural factors as they affect the results of mental testing upon Negroes," Harris wrote on June 22, 1928. "I told him you are interested in the same thing or something similar to it."[31] On June 23, 1928, Thompson himself wrote to Boas; Harris, he said, had suggested that he write "with the possible idea of effecting some sort of cooperation." Thompson wanted some specific information: "Granting the fact that the results of intelligence and educational tests are conditioned by environment, and I think recent investigations show that we must grant this fact— a. How may this influence be measured, and b. What are the results of such measurements?"[32] Boas's reply of July 5, 1928, however, indicated only that he would "be very glad to hear . . . about the work" Thompson was doing.[33]

Boas seemed more willing to reveal some aspects of his project when Howard Hale Long contacted him on March 13, 1929. Long had been informed by Abram Harris that Boas was "preparing some mental tests for pupils with varying cultural backgrounds." "I am quite sure," Long added, "that I do not wholly understand what your program is, but for some time the conclusion has been forcing itself upon me that the current mental tests are not suitable in some respects, for a large number of Negro children."[34] In his reply of March 18, Boas indicated that he was "trying to get in detail the social background of individual children and . . . intending to work out a psychological test on the basis of this information." He did not expect that he could "give any kind of definite information until about the end of the present calendar year."[35] What happened to Boas's unbiased mental test is a mystery. There are no indications either that it was widely administered to persons of varying social backgrounds or that it demonstrated significantly different results for African Americans.

Boas was even more skeptical of the validity of blood group tests than intelligence tests in reflecting the genetic structure of "races." Some anthropologists thought blood tests, which had been used to substantiate racist arguments before the 1920s, were the bases for determining historical relationships between the races. When Monroe N. Work, as director of the Division of Records and Research at Tuskegee Institute, asked Boas on June 14, 1920, if "race mixture" could be determined by blood tests,

Boas replied on July 13, 1920: "In case of strong admixture of white blood I would not want to determine whether any one has negro blood or not."[36]

In short, although his replies to African Americans were often curt, Boas was throughout his career a source of support for those who wanted to recontextualize the conclusions of the dominant discourse of scientific racism; despite his ambivalences about their purported defective heritage, he was a friend of the African American intelligentsia.

His relationship with Zora Neale Hurston is most revealing of this empathetic side. Boas had initially met Hurston at Barnard College when she was an undergraduate majoring in anthropology. During the two summers before her graduation from Barnard, Hurston assisted Melville J. Herskovits in a project that Boas had conceived, measuring the bodily forms of Harlemites. In 1927, after considerable wrangling, Boas obtained a fellowship of $1,400 for Hurston from Carter G. Woodson, the founder of the Association for the Study of Negro Life and History; she was to solicit and collect folklore in Florida.[37]

Hurston's first venture at collecting folklore was unsuccessful. Although Boas thought Hurston had made a valiant effort, he wrote to her on May 3, 1927: "I find that what you obtained is very largely repetition of the kind of material that has been collected so much." Before she had begun the research, Boas had asked her "to pay attention, not so much to the content, but rather to the form of diction." Having modified his 1909 position on African retentions, he believed that "in transmission from Africa to America most of the contents of the culture have been adopted from the surrounding peoples while the mannerisms have to a great extent, been retained." In the particular case of singing, Boas went on to point out, "When you compare Negro singing and the singing of white people, it is not so much musical notation that is different, but rather the manner of rendition." Furthermore, he thought it was necessary for Hurston to draw cultural distinctions between African Americans, "to compare the superstitious beliefs that occur among the Spanish and French speaking Negroes."[38]

After returning from the South, during the early fall of 1927, Hurston became acquainted with Charlotte van der Veer Quick, a patron of such African American intellectuals as Langston Hughes, Alain LeRoy Locke, Miguel Covarrubias, Aaron Douglas, and Richmond Barthe. Over the next five years, "Godmother" or "Mrs. Mason" as she was called by her clientele contributed approximately $15,000 to Hurston's project of collecting the folklore of rural southern blacks. Hurston began her second collection tour in Mobile, Alabama, in December 1927 and went on from there. According to her biographer, Robert E. Hemenway, the next few years "were exciting, stimulating years. They provided Hurston with a lifetime of folk material to draw on, even though her fame was not established until her material was published in the mid-thirties."[39]

After a tour in Alabama and Florida, Hurston went to New Orleans in August 1928 and began collecting materials there. In December she sent Boas a box of oranges; in return he implored her to write him from "time to time."[40] Two days after Christmas, Hurston wrote Boas that Mrs. Mason had "exacted" the promise "of me that I write *no one*." Yet Hurston insisted that she had "intended from the very beginning to show you what I have, but after I had returned." She went on to criticize Howard W. Odum and Guy B. Johnson, whose books she thought were "in error constantly. A too hasty generalization." After telling Boas that she was looking into the "subject of sympathetic magic . . . as thoroughly as I can," and also indicating that she remembered Boas's interest in Creole languages, she thanked him for "the experience I had under you, [it] was a splendid foundation."[41]

Boas's allegiance to Hurston seemed to grow as time passed. On May 17, 1929, he wrote her that he and Otto Klineberg were doing investigations into "mental characteristics of various groups," with the intention of attempting "to establish certain psychological tests which are particularly well fitted to different cultural groups." In particular, he was interested in developing "a test of music in which the special ability of the Negroes in this direction might play an important role and we want to find a place where we may get information in regard to individual attitudes towards music, interest in music, and musical ability." Boas offered Hurston $150 a month for four months to work on the project under Klineberg's supervision.[42]

But even though Hurston wanted to work for Boas and Klineberg, and her contract with Mrs. Mason was about to expire, the "Godmother" held the rights on her material, and Hurston wanted to get that two years' collection into print. She did spend some time in New Orleans in October 1929 with Klineberg, but their attempts to find a "singing" community had disappointing results. In fact, Klineberg wrote to Boas: "Evidently Miss Hurston didn't quite understand what we wanted, although I did my best to make it very clear." He added:

> On the musical side the Negroes of New Orleans seem to be interesting more because in the churches and in the homes there is some fine singing of spirituals by a number of gifted adults who are really creative in their singing, and who, according to Miss Hurston, interpret the spirituals better than Robeson or Hayes or the others [with] whom white people are familiar. That is of course interesting, and I shall certainly look into it as carefully as I can, but it is not just what I wanted. There are many communities (I know of some in North

Carolina . . .) where everybody sings and where the "culture" would definitely be oriented in that direction. I understood that Miss Hurston was taking me to such a community, and in that respect I was rather disappointed.[43]

Despite Klineberg's coolness towards Hurston, Boas continued his amicable support of her in the 1930s. When she asked him to write an introduction to her book of folklore titled *Mules and Men*, Boas "promised to write one if the manuscript is of the character that would seem to me desirable."[44] He must have found it so, because his one-page "Preface" appeared in her book when it was published in 1935. In it Boas noted that Hurston possessed an insider's perspective that enabled her to penetrate "the affected demeanor by which the Negro excluded the White observer effectively from participating in his true inner life"; her book was an "unusual contribution to our knowledge of the true inner life of the Negro." For students of "culture history," like himself, the work was not only particularly satisfying in "giving the Negro's reaction to everyday events, to his emotional life, his humor and passion," but particularly insightful for those who compared African American culture and European tradition. Boas argued that this hypothesis was "important for understanding historically the character of American Negro life, with its strong African background in the West Indies, the importance of which diminishes with increasing distance from the south."[45]

Hurston also wanted Boas to support her pursuit of a graduate degree in anthropology at Columbia University: "I really do feel the discipline in research and I want to use this grant of money to that end. I might want to teach some day and I want the degree as well as the discipline for thoroughness." But she became embroiled in a dispute with the paternalistic president of the Rosenwald Foundation, Edwin Embree, concerning the dispensation of her fellowship and left Columbia in the spring of 1935. There had been a plan for her to spend a year from spring 1935 to spring 1936 taking courses in ethnology and studying Haiti with Melville Herskovits at Northwestern University in Evanston, Illinois and she had written Boas on January 4, 1935: "I'll cheerfully go to Evanston if you think that is best for me. Perhaps Dr. Herskovits can with my feeble contribution work out something that would help others who wish to study the American Negro as well as me."[46] And Herskovits, who had received a letter from Hurston that same month, was sympathetic; he wrote Boas on January 18, 1935: "If she does turn up, I am sure that it will be possible to train her in such a way that she will be able to organize the enormous amount of information she possesses."[47] Nevertheless, mortgaging her future in academia for short-term celebrity status, Hurston left Columbia without ever notifying Boas. In April 1935, Boas was asking Hurston to "come in" to talk with him in reference to her plan of study.[48]

Boas had exhibited more ambivalence toward Alain LeRoy Locke than toward Hurston. Locke, chairman of the Department of Philosophy at Howard University between 1917 and 1925, was fired from that position in order, according to the philosopher Leonard Harris, "to reduce the power of forces pursuing equitable pay between blacks and whites," sought Boas's support.[49] On December 3, 1925, Locke wrote Boas, requesting an investigation of his firing by a committee of the American Association of University Professors (AAUP).[50] Two days later Boas wrote the president of the association that Locke and three of his colleagues had been "summarily dismissed" and that there had been "no previous intimation of the possibility of dismissal or definite official notice of charges of inefficiency or misconduct, and according to the official letter of notification the grounds given were 'economy and reorganization.'"[51] As a result of Boas's letter and the action of the AAUP, Locke and his colleagues were paid their full salaries for one year though they were not reinstated.[52]

Yet despite having rendered this assistance, Boas refused to support Locke's bid the following year for a fellowship from Carter G. Woodson's Association for the Study of Negro Life and History. On November 16, 1926, Woodson wrote Boas: "Kindly inform me frankly whether you feel that this study properly comes within the purview of what we planned to do in anthropology or whether we can justly use our anthropology fund to finance a study of this sort."[53] The proposal Locke had submitted, which Woodson forwarded to Boas, read as follows:

> My plan would be to undertake directly a study of AFRICAN ART AS AN EXPRESSION (or INDEX) of AFRICAN CULTURE, but in reading through the quite voluminous literature (see attached Bibliography) to take notes and citations covering the broader field of the cultural values of the African civilizations in so far as social customs or social philosophy reflected in folk-lore, religious or social beliefs, or institutional practice might give clues to these values. Especially in the field of art symbols and their closely related religious conceptions, I believe we have the only available clues left to the moot question of the antiquity and indigenous character of certain supposedly African contributions to early civilization. (The basis of interpretation and the line of investigation here would be that boldly suggested by the Flinders Petrie school of comparative cultural anthropology, and an article of Wainwright on African survivals and Egyptian Art in ANCIENT EGYPT, 1916.)

My present anticipation is that such notes and citations would form the basis of a much more extensive treatise on AFRICAN CULTURE ORIGINS in the course of a year or so of research reading.

I would be willing on part or whole time basis to undertake such a program November 15, 1926.

Note: I have seen the principal collections of African art, at Brussels, London, the Pitt-Rivers private Museum. Berlin Institute of Ethnology, Hamburg, Dresden, Frankfort on Main, the British Museum, the Barnes Foundation Collection, the University of Pennsylvania Museum, the Ward Collection (Smithsonian), and have available for private study the Blondiau Collection of Dushongo and Congo Art, which I located and had purchased by Mrs. Edith Isaacs of Theatre Arts. Though these might in certain instances need to be revisited, the main work for the present could be done from my own notes on these collections and the museum catalogues, several of which are available.[54]

After reading Locke's proposal, Boas indicated to Woodson on November 18 that he knew Locke "personally" and thought "a good deal of him" but could not "endorse his plan which does not seem to be well conceived." Furthermore, he stated candidly, "I do not think it possible to make a study that would be a valuable contribution in the space of one year and without prolonged studies in European museums."[55]

Woodson immediately conferred with Locke and in a tone of partisanship for Locke wrote Boas on November 19, 1926: "What you say about Doctor A.L. Locke I shall consider very serious." But "I should add," he continued, apparently trying to nudge Boas from his steadfast position, "that Doctor Locke will be glad to study in Europe two or three years if you consider the plan feasible. The main point . . . is to determine whether or not such a study is worthwhile and whether or not he can do it."[56] Yet Boas held adamantly to his original position: "The proposal of Dr. Locke of course would be quite different if he were willing to continue it for several years. As it is now I do not think it is possible; besides this I do not know whether he has the general ethnological knowledge which would be necessary to carry through a plan of this kind."[56] As a consequence of this letter to Woodson, Locke did not receive the fellowship; it was awarded instead to Zora Neale Hurston.

Boas was far more supportive of Abram L. Harris, who would emerge as a leading economist at Howard University in the 1930s. On May 14, 1923, when Woodson was searching for a candidate for a fellowship in anthropological and psychological research, Boas tentatively suggested Harris: "I doubt whether he is just the ideal man for this position, but he makes a good impression, and I should be willing to risk it."[57] Woodson was not favorably impressed, however, and told Boas frankly on May 15: "I am hoping that a better man than Mr. Harris can be found."[58]

Boas continued his attempt to get funding for Harris in 1926 and 1927, but to no avail.[59] In the end there was only bad blood between Woodson and Harris, as is obvious in a letter from Harris to Boas of February 26, 1930: "Do you recall the study of 'Negro Business Enterprise' that I planned while working for you, and which you sought to have Dr. G. Woodson finance? I am trying to revive it, although I see that Dr. Woodson has himself just published a study of the 'Negro Business Man.' Whatever stimulus my plans of three years ago gave him does not matter since his product is not what I wished to turn out."[60]

Boas's support of various young African American intellectuals led some of them to be supportive of him when the crisis in Europe took place during the mid-1930s. For example, Abram L. Harris wrote Boas on October 9, 1936, during the French Groupe D'Étude et D'Information "Races et Racisme" international congress in Paris: "Professor Lips told me of the Paris meeting and the dominance of the Nazis at it. Shame on the French. Let's hope that we can have an International Congress soon which will be a powerful antidote to these racialists and the concomitant hatred that they inspire."[61] On December 20, 1938, George Edmund Haynes thanked Boas for "the statement given from the many scientists who responded to your call for their word against the rising tide of prejudice and hatred that is coming out of Germany."[62] Despite the support of African Americans and others, however, Boas would go to his grave in anguish, suffering a fatal heart attack while denouncing Nazi propaganda in 1942.

To conclude, although there are grounds to infer that Boas was deflecting charges of subjectivism by not attacking anti-Semitism—which adversely affected his career during the 1880s and early 1890s—and focusing on antiblack racism instead, the preponderance of historical evidence suggests that he was genuinely concerned with the problem of solving America's dilemma. In short, he was committed to using every means at his disposal for African American uplift.

3

The Myths of Africa in the Writings of Booker T. Washington

Since the 1960s, several scholars examining the discourses between white American elites on the character and capabilities of African Americans, though cognizant of the exceptionalism of Franz Boas, have branded American thinkers during the Progressive era as racists[1]—especially those in the disciplines which in 1915 the distinguished anthropologist of the Native Americans, Alfred L. Kroeber, called "history": historical anthropology, history proper, and sociology.[2] Recent scholars have certainly told the truth about their forebears in those disciplines but not the whole truth, for they have virtually ignored the participation of African Americans in the discourses.

Racial thought in the age of Booker T. Washington is marked at one end by the 1883 publication of George Washington Williams's *History of the Negro Race from 1619 to 1880: Negroes as Slaves, Soldiers, and as Citizens,* and at the other by Washington's death in 1915. During those years the destructive notion that African Americans were the descendants of barbarous peoples and therefore capable of progress only under the Christian and civilizing influences of whites, was the dominant mythology of liberal blacks and whites alike. It was an evolutionary naturalistic mythology created through a cluster of tales told about the past which legitimized past and contemporaneous relations between blacks and whites and held out the possibility of the progressive evolution of blacks only in the distant future.[3]

During the first decade of the twentieth century, however, a varied group of black and white liberal, moderate, and conservative intellectuals—such as Franz Boas (who influenced Monroe N. Work and Robert E. Park) and James H. Breasted—held that African Americans were the descendants of peoples who had made in the past, and were perfectly capable of making in the present and future, achievements essential to human progress. These thinkers who came of age during the 1890s told scientific, naturalistic tales that reinforced one another and formed the historical element in the attempt to discredit the status quo in white-black relations. In so doing, they created internal conceptual stresses in the historical disciplines on the issue of the capabilities of the "Negro." Although their mythology would not become the dominant one in "history" until after 1930—when new social problems were brought about by the Great Depression and by the migration of many blacks from the South into the urban-industrial North—they influenced as early as the first decade of the twentieth century the thought of Booker T. Washington, W.E.B. Du Bois, and George Washington Ellis. These mythographers thereby transformed mainstream African American thought on the capabilities of Africans from one that reflected the dominant attitudes of the society at large to some of the most progressive attitudes on that issue during the period from 1909 until 1930.

George Washington Williams was a native of Bedford Springs, Pennsylvania; he had served in the Union Army during the Civil War, had graduated from Newton Theological Seminary, and was an ordained Baptist minister; he was also the first black member of the Ohio state legislature. Like many members of the African American elite and the dominant white elite of British ancestry of this period, Williams was intent on creating in effect a myth of the "Guinea Negro" and slavery which would serve to rationalize the reconciliation between North and South that had taken place since 1877. He wrote:

> [The] antiquity of the Negro race is beyond dispute. This is a fact established by the most immutable historical data, and recorded on the monumental brass and marble of the Oriental nations of the most remote period of time. The importance and worth of the Negro have given him a place in all the histories of Egypt, Greece and Rome. His position, it is true, in all history up to the present day, has been accidental, incidental, and collateral; but it is sufficient to show how he has been regarded in the past by other nations. His brightest days were when history was an infant; and, since he early turned from God, he has found the cold face of hate and the hurtful hand of the Caucasian against him. The Negro type is the result of degradation. It is nothing more than the lowest strata of the African race. Pouring over the venerable mountain terraces, an abundant stream from an abundant and unknown source into the malarial districts, the genuine African has gradually degenerated into the typical Negro. His blood infected with the poison of his low habitation, his body shriveled by disease, his intellect veiled in pagan superstitions, the noblest yearnings of his soul strangled at birth by the savage passions of a nature abandoned to sensuality,—the poor Negro of Africa deserved more our pity than our contempt.
>
> It is true that the weaker tribes, or many of the Negroid type, were the chief source of supply for the slave-market in this country for many years; but slavery in the United States—a severe ordeal through which to pass to citizenship and civilization—had the effect of calling into life many a slumbering and dying attribute in the Negro nature. The cruel

institution drove him from an extreme idolatry to an extreme religious exercise of his faith in worship. And now that he is an American citizen,—the condition and circumstances which rendered his piety appropriate abolished,—to move over to an extreme rationalism.[4]

The passage reflects the quandary in which Williams found himself; he was caught between the proslavery myths of the ante-bellum "American school" of ethnology and the southern Comteans on one hand, and the liberation myths of the African American elites on the other. Like the former two groups, Williams held that slavery had been—to use their terms—a "positive good" that had transformed the mentally enervated, pagan "Negroid type" into a Christian and somewhat civilized being. Like the African American proponents of "Ethiopianism," Williams believed—as Professor Wilson Jeremiah Moses has put it—that it was the "destiny of black people to create an exemplary civilization . . . in Africa, but not only there." And like all three groups, Williams believed in "civilization": that is, "that Africans would be uplifted and redeemed in proportion to the[ir] acceptance of European civilization."[5] Much to his dismay, however, Williams would witness the subordination of blacks in the South and the exploitation of Africa by the European powers during the 1880s. By 1900 the United States and Europe alike were united behind the banner of white supremacy.

It is within this context of increasing racial proscription that a group of articulate mythographers emerged, including Booker T. Washington, Daniel G. Brinton, Joseph A. Tillinghast, and Jerome Dowd, to tell tales about African Americans that rationalized the virulent racism of Americans of British ancestry. The major myths of African inferiority, the civilizing effects of slavery, the horrors of Reconstruction, and the gradual uplift of blacks through industrial education were interwoven sophistically and infiltrated "history." It was at the end of this development that Ulrich Bonnell Phillips, using the myth of African inferiority—the keystone of the proslavery and Jim Crow arguments—sought to provide the historical element in the political mythology of those members of the elite who were attempting to rationalize white-black relations in the Progressive era. Fortunately, when Phillips's book was published in 1918, that era had just passed; it had been shattered, metaphorically speaking, by World War I, by thousands of Southern black migrants on railway cars heading to the urban-industrial North, and by the work of scholars such as Franz Boas who questioned the racist assumptions that underlay Phillips's analysis.[6]

Ironically, it was the ex-slave, self-made man, and educator Booker T. Washington who, at the height of his influence, adumbrated the political mythology most frequently used to justify turn-of-the-century race relations; he did so in order to rationalize his program of the gradual uplift of blacks through industrial education. On September 18, 1895, the principal of Tuskegee Normal and Industrial Institute delivered an address to a mixed audience at the opening of the Atlanta Cotton States and International Exposition. Then thirty-nine years old, Washington had spent his first nine years of life as a slave and had witnessed the "peculiar institution's" demise. He had also lived through the period when the North attempted to reconstruct the South; he had seen the reconciliation between two great sections take place in 1877; and he bore witness to the subordination of blacks in the South after Reconstruction. Disenfranchisement by amended state constitutions had occurred in Mississippi in 1890 and was taking place in South Carolina at the time of Washington's address in 1895. Through the gradual proliferation of Jim Crow laws, extralegal violence, and the removal of blacks from positions in skilled labor—all aided and abetted by the unethical political climate in the South—whites had consolidated their higher-caste positions over blacks.

Although he did not mention specific names, Washington began his address by scolding black emigrationists, "who depend on bettering their condition in a foreign land," and those militant blacks "who underestimate the importance of cultivating friendly relations with the Southern white man as his next-door neighbor." The ex-slave's interpretation of black history stressed the idea that blacks had been loyal servants to the whites, "nursing your children, watching by the sick bed of your mothers and fathers, and often following them with tear-dimmed eyes to their graves." Revealing his nativist thought, Washington argued that whites "who look to the incoming of those of foreign birth and strange tongue and habits for the prosperity of the South" had a "limited knowledge of the black contribution to Southern history." For "without strikes and labour wars," blacks had "tilled your fields, cleared your forests, built your railroads and cities, and brought forth treasures from the bowels of the earth." Nevertheless, whatever the monumental role they had played in the antebellum achievements of the South, blacks were not prepared for the coming of industrialization. During Reconstruction, Washington asserted, "ignorant and inexperienced" blacks "began at the top instead of at the bottom." For them "a seat in Congress or the state legislature was more sought than real estate or industrial skill . . . [and] the convention of stump speaking had more attractions than starting a dairy farm or truck garden."[7]

In effect, Washington exonerated white southerners of responsibility for the so-called Negro problem and placed it squarely on the shoulders of blacks. Learning the virtues of common labor, he believed, would yield far more gains than politics. In regard to the role of blacks in the South's economy, he suggested that some would find a place in the professions, but for the overwhelming number, Washington asserted, "it is at the bottom of life we must begin, and not at the top."[8]

Sociologically speaking, he envisioned a South where there would be great social distance between blacks and whites ("In all things that are purely social we can be as separate as the fingers") yet considerable inter-group collaboration ("one as the hand in all things essential to mutual progress"). Projecting the social Darwinist mind-set with its emphasis on the "survival of the fittest," and a buoyant spirit of optimism, the Tuskegee Wizard argued that African Americans would eventually achieve equality not by agitation for social equality but by a "severe and constant struggle" in the marketplace.[9]

Historical interpretations implying that Washington's Atlanta Exposition address either soothed the consciences of the justices of the Supreme Court that legitimized Jim Crow laws in *Plessy v. Ferguson* (1896) or was an expedient strategy have generated heated scholarly debates. Those debates, however, seem unresolvable—especially when the adversaries take into account the virulent racism that pervaded the nation and Washington's surreptitious struggle against the forces of reaction in the South.[10] In any case, Washington's ideas deserve close scrutiny, for he was more than a mere "man of action"; he was a consummate mythmaker. When "history" eventually discredited his mythology, this thoughtful, reflective man modified some of his myths but left others intact.

On May 19, 1931, in a lecture before his University of Chicago sociology course titled "The Negro in America," Robert Ezra Park outlined the social philosophy of Booker T. Washington. Park, who had served as a ghostwriter for Washington from 1905 to 1913, and who was the most distinguished student of race relations in the country, asserted that Washington "really represented" the freedman who wanted to attain first-class citizenship. Unlike the aristocratic W.E.B. Du Bois—who represented educated blacks and in the tradition of the abolitionists appealed to "rights" in the Fourteenth and Fifteenth Amendments to the Constitution in an attempt to make existing laws operative—Washington thought that whites believed it was their "right and duty to keep" the African American "in his place."

Drawing on William Graham Sumner, a conservative social Darwinist whose concept of "the mores" encouraged what the late Swedish political economist Gunnar Myrdal called a "laissez faire, do-nothing" approach to white-black relations, Park argued that Washington knew that the subordination of African Americans "was deep in the mores of the South." Furthermore, Park suggested, Washington "realized and knew" that effective laws "must rest" on mores and customs and that as a consequence, "in order to make laws operative," both whites and blacks would have to be "reeducated"—"particularly the whites." By changing the "sound, natural conditions which made the mores what they were," one could "then change the mores." Thus, Washington's philosophy of gradual economic uplift through industrial education was, according to Park, set up to "reeducate" African Americans in the South for a new system of labor in which, unlike slavery, the black masses were supposed to "find work dignifying . . . a privilege." Park asserted that the "purpose of Washington's education was to convince [the] negro that he could do things. Start him on *his own*."[11]

Washington believed that providing African Americans in the South with an industrial education could provide the impetus for transforming the mores of whites. Park interpreted Washington's philosophy of community in *agape*-like terms: "Washington [was] always saying that both white and black have a community of interest. [Washington] didn't appeal to mores, or law, but to the individual. If [the blacks] don't get justice, it reacts back on the whole community. . . . His appeal [was] that interests of negro and white were alike [and] would lead to laws that protect both alike."[12]

Despite what seemed like a sane social philosophy, at the height of his influence, it should be stressed that Washington publicly used the political mythology most frequently promulgated to justify turn-of-the-century race relations in order to rationalize his program of the gradual economic advance of African Americans in the South through industrial education. In his autobiography, *Up from Slavery*, which sold 30,000 copies between its initial publication in 1901 and September 1903, Washington implied that African Americans were the descendants of barbarous peoples and therefore capable of progress only under the Christian and civilizing influences of whites. He then joined the themes of African primitiveness and the civilizing effects of slavery:

> When we rid ourselves of prejudice, or racial feeling, and look facts in the face, we must acknowledge that, not withstanding the cruelty and moral wrong of slavery, the ten million Negroes inhabiting this country, who themselves or whose ancestors went through the school of American slavery, are in a stronger and more hopeful condition materially, intellectually, morally, and religiously than is true of an equal number of black people in any portion of the globe. This is [true] to such an extent that Negroes in this country, who themselves or whose forefathers went through the school of slavery, are constantly returning to Africa to enlighten those who remain in the fatherland.[13]

Washington's ghostwriter S. Laing Williams, a prominent African American who practiced law in Chicago, was even more emphatic about the progressiveness of Anglo-Americans and the primitiveness of African blacks when he wrote in a biography of Frederick Douglass in 1907: "The chance or destiny which brought to this land of ours, and placed in the midst of the most progressive and most enlightened race that Christian civilization has produced, some three or four millions of primitive black people from Africa and their descendants, has created one of the most interesting and difficult social problems which any modern people has had to face."[14]

To today's reader Washington's and Williams's statements may well seem little more than a rationalization for the status quo. But it must be remembered that their defense of the institution of slavery and the limited progress of African Americans was a moderate position. Other intellectuals such as General Francis A. Walker, James Bryce, Joseph Le Conte, Eugene Rollin Carson, Joseph A. Tillinghast, Paul B. Barringer, Frederick L. Hoffman, and Walter F. Willcox argued that African Americans were degenerating and predicted that they would become extinct. These spokesmen for black degeneracy, as George M. Fredrickson has correctly pointed out, were Darwinians to whom it seemed logical that "if the blacks were a degenerating race with no future, the problem ceased to be one of how to prepare them for citizenship or even how to make them more productive and useful members of the community. The new prognosis pointed rather to the need to segregate or quarantine a race liable to be a source of contamination and social danger to the white community, as it sank even deeper into the slough of disease, vice, and criminality."[15]

It is true that Washington was a social Darwinist of a sort—insofar as his philosophy was primarily materialistic—but he did not exclude moral or religious forces in accounting for the evolution of humans. For example, he wrote in *The Negro in the South* in 1907:

> I sometimes fear that in our great anxiety to push forward we lay too much stress upon our former condition. We should think less of our former growth and more of the present and of the things which go to retard or hinder that growth. In one of his letters to the Galatians, St. Paul says: "But the fruit of the spirit is love, joy, peace, long-suffering, gentleness, goodness, faith, temperance; against such there is no law."
>
> I believe that it is possible for a race, as it is for an individual, to learn to live up in such a high atmosphere that there is no human law that can prevail against it. There is no man who can pass a law to affect the Negro in relation to his singing, his peace, and his self-control. Wherever I go I would enter St. Paul's atmosphere and, living through and in that spirit, we will grow and make progress and, notwithstanding discouragements and mistakes we will become an increasingly strong part of the Christian citizenship of this republic.[16]

In addition to disagreeing with the Darwinians concerning a Supreme Being or purpose in the universe, Washington disagreed with them on the question of the potency of human agency or will. His embrace of neo-Lamarckianism suggested that will or purpose could and did bring about evolutionary change; that is, the idea of the inheritance of acquired characteristics suggested that not only bad behavior but good behavior could be transmitted from one generation to another. Washington used the principle to insist that the purported differences between the races were not permanent: "It is only through struggle and the surmounting of difficulties that races, like individuals, are made strong, powerful, and useful."[17]

As early as 1899, in *The Future of the American Negro*, Washington had clearly drawn a distinction between his position and that of intellectuals who believed in the impending extinction of blacks: "A few people predicted that freedom would result disastrously to the Negro, as far as numerical increase was concerned; but so far the census figures have failed to bear out this prediction. . . . It is my opinion that the rate of increase in the future will be still greater than it has been from the close of the war of the Rebellion up to the present time, for the reason that the very sudden changes which took place in the life of the Negro because of his freedom, plunged him into many excesses that were detrimental to his physical well-being."[18] He had had grave doubts, for example, about the period of Reconstruction, during which "two ideas were constantly agitating the minds of colored people, or, at least, the minds of the larger part of the race. One of these was the craze for Greek and Latin learning, and the other was a desire to hold office." The fascination of African Americans with such status and power symbols, Washington argued, should have been expected from "a people who had spent generations in slavery and generations before that in the darkest heathenism."[19]

Yet the desire of African Americans to learn classical languages and to hold political office were not the most serious flaws that Washington detected in the defunct era of Reconstruction. His major grievance centered on the maternal relationship between the government and its African American wards: "During the whole of the Reconstruction period our people throughout the South looked to the Federal Government for everything, very much as a child looks to its mother. This was not unnatural. The central government gave them freedom, and the whole Nation had been enriched for more than two centuries by the labour of the Negro. Even as a youth, and later in manhood, I had the feeling that it was cruelly wrong in the central government, at the beginning of our freedom, to fail to make provision for the general education of our people in addition to what the states might do, so that the people would be the better prepared for the duties of citizenship."[20]

It would be a mistake to argue that Washington was wholly critical of Reconstruction; in 1899 he wrote that it had "served at least to show the world that with proper preparation and with a sufficient foundation the Negro possesses the elements out of which men of the highest character and usefulness can be developed."[21] Two years later he stated emphatically that "not all coloured people who were in office during Reconstruction were unworthy of their positions by any means. Some of them, like the late Senator B.K. Bruce, Governor Pinchback, and many others, were strong, upright, useful men."[22] The problem, according to Washington, was not race but too little education and experience. Therefore, Washington recommended basing the franchise of both blacks and whites on property and educational qualifications. These "tests," he thought, "should be made to apply honestly and squarely to both the white and black races."[23]

In short, in 1901 Washington viewed the vast majority of Africans and African Americans as barbarous underachievers who were not yet able to attain the heights of civilization reached by Anglo-Americans. His solution to the problems of African Americans was industrial education. Through "education of the hand, head, and heart"—in other words, by becoming acculturated—Washington believed African Americans could eventually contribute to the markets of the world and become prepared to exercise first-class citizenship.

To comprehend the essence of Washington's philosophy of gradual uplift through industrial education, one must examine the social and intellectual influences that made the idea seem a positive good and therefore a solution to problems deriving from the economic arrangements that differentiated most blacks from most whites in the South. The concept of industrial education had its origins in the educational theories of Europeans such as Johann Pestalozzi and Philipp von Fellenberg, but its emphasis on morality, thrift, industry, economic independence, and material success—according to August Meier—had taken hold in the United States as early as the 1820s. The idea that some youth should acquire a trade or mechanical training arose during the Negro Convention movement as a result of the exclusion of blacks from the skilled trades. As early as 1831, the Philadelphia Convention proposed "that a college be established at New Haven as soon as $20,000 are obtained, and to be on the Manual Labour System, by which in connexion with a scientific education they [Young Men of Colour] may also obtain a useful Mechanical or Agricultural progression." The conventions of the 1830s and 1840s continued (to no avail, however) to adopt plans for potential manual trade schools. In fact, at a convention in 1848 a committee of five which included Frederick Douglass stated that "every blow of the sledge hammer, wielded by a sable arm, is a powerful blow in support of our cause. Every colored mechanic, is by virtue of circumstances an elevator of his race. . . . Trades are important. Whenever a man may be thrown by misfortune, if he has in his hands a useful trade, he is useful to his fellow man, and will be esteemed accordingly."[24]

The mistaken notion that a black man or woman who had a useful trade would be esteemed and treated accordingly was sustained from 1860 through the 1890s by the Freedmen's Bureau commissioners, missionary schoolteachers, Methodists, and the American Missionary Association, the last of which helped to create the most successful agricultural and industrial school for blacks before 1890: Hampton Institute in Virginia. It was at Hampton under General Samuel Chapman Armstrong, who regarded industrial education as a moral force, that Booker T. Washington was trained. In his last address, delivered before the American Missionary Association and the National Council of Congregational Churches in New Haven, Connecticut, on October 25, 1915, Washington celebrated "a transformation" that had been "wrought to my race since the landing at Jamestown and the landing of the last slaves at Mobile," a transformation involving "growth in numbers, mental awakening, self-support, securing of property, moral and religious development, and adjustment of relations between relations. To what in a single generation are we more indebted for this transformation in the direction of a higher civilization than the American Missionary Association?"[25]

Industrial education, as Meier has astutely pointed out, could be viewed as either "a means for helping the laboring classes to rise in the world," or "as a type of instruction suitable for adjusting them to their social role." It is not clear which function Washington truly believed it served, but historical hindsight has demonstrated that his optimism contained a greater degree of falsity than truth. "The fact remains," wrote C. Vann Woodward in 1951, "that Washington's training school, and the many schools he inspired taught crafts and attitudes more congenial to the pre-machine age than to the twentieth century."[26]

Having publicly embraced the myth of African inferiority and the "positive good" of slavery, Washington could and would not admit that his program of gradual uplift through industrial education might be a sham. In 1907, at the end of this period in his development, he wrote:

> In his native country, owing to climatic conditions, and also because of his few simple and crude wants, the Negro, before coming to America, had little necessity to labor. You have, perhaps, read the story, that it is said might be true in certain portions of Africa, of how the native simply lies down on his back under a banana-tree and falls asleep with

his mouth open. The banana falls into his mouth while he is asleep and he wakes ups and finds that all he has to do is to chew it—he has his meal already served.

Notwithstanding the fact that, in most cases, the element of compulsion entered into the labor of the slave, and the main object sought was the enrichment of the owner, the American Negro had, under the regime of slavery, his first lesson in anything like continuous progressive, systematic labor.[27]

Washington's myth of African inferiority attracted most social scientists in "history." And although the Boasian position of equipotentiality (in reference to West and Central Africans) surfaced in 1904 and would influence most prominent sociologists and anthropologists in the field of race relations by 1929, the myth of African inferiority in history proper sustained itself for forty more years.

The myth was not static, however. Louis R. Harlan has correctly pointed out that Washington's version in particular was dynamic, given the "growing knowledge of African history and the new ideas of anthropology, sociology, and archaeology." Influenced by Franz Boas, Monroe N. Work, Robert E. Park, and James H. Breasted, Washington was not merely "a man of action" but a thoughtful, reflective person who slowly modified his views until they conformed to the most recent and authoritative findings in the social sciences.

In 1904, when he was seeking to diversify the racial composition of students in American anthropology, Boas requested Booker T. Washington's advice concerning the admission of James Emman Kwegyr Aggrey to graduate study in anthropology at Columbia University. Aggrey, a Fanti (born in the Gold Coast) who had received a B.A. at Livingston College in 1902, Boas wrote, "is a full-blood negro and so far as I can learn, his standing is such that he will require at least one year of undergraduate work before he can be admitted to university. . . . From what I hear from my colleagues who made his acquaintance at the session of the summer school, he is a very bright man. He is, however, without means, and will require support in order to complete his studies. I do not know whether it would be possible to obtain this support here in the city, but I do not think it is unlikely."[28]

Nevertheless, Boas clearly labored when he considered the dismal career prospects that Aggrey would face once he had satisfactorily completed the requirements for an advanced degree. "I very much hesitate to advise the young man to take up this work, because I fear that it would be very difficult after he has completed his studies to find a place," he wrote.

"On the other hand, it might perhaps be possible for him to study for two or three years and to take his degree of master of arts, and then to obtain a position in one of the higher schools established for his race. I feel that the matter is a rather delicate one, and I do not wish to advise the young man or to assist him in beginning a study which may ultimately put him in a most unfortunate position."[29] Though extremely pessimistic about Aggrey's employment prospects, Boas did have one suggestion: "It is of course evident that if he developed into a good scientist, he could do excellent work particularly in Africa, which would be of the greatest service to science. This is a consideration which makes me desirous of assisting him. . . . Perhaps by proper application, and if he were the right man, it might be possible to get him into Colonial service of one of the European countries that have colonies in Africa."[30]

That Boas's liberalism in 1904 was far too progressive for the leading black spokesman of the period—who believed that blacks needed to enter the practical vocations—is reflected in Washington's response:

> Judging by what you state in your letter and knowing what I do, I can not rid myself of the feeling that the course which he is planning to take will be of little value to him. At the present time I know of so many cases where young colored men and women would have done well had they thoroughly prepared themselves for teachers, some kind of work in the industries, or in the applied sciences, but instead, they have made the mistake of taking a course that had no practical bearing on the needs of the race; the result being they ended up as hotel-waiters or Pullman car porters.[31]

Aggrey went on to receive an M.A. from Livingston College in 1912, a D.D. degree from Hood Theological Seminary, and an M.A. from Columbia University in 1922. He became a member of the Phelps-Stokes Committee on Education in Africa during the early 1920s and eventually served as vice-principal of Achimota Prince of Wales College and School in present-day Ghana. Still, as Boas would later learn, the Tuskegee Wizard was no man's fool; his statements had some basis in empirical reality—especially when one considers the career of Zora Neale Hurston almost three decades later. Her biographer has shown that even Boas, who helped Hurston draw up a plan for her doctoral program, was unable to gain long-term support for her—despite her status as the author of a novel and a book of folklore.[32]

On November 8, 1906, Boas wrote to Booker T. Washington, asking to speak with him when he came to the Carl Schurz Memorial Meeting in New York City. Boas indicated that he was "endeavoring to organize certain scientific work on the Negro race" which he believed would be "of great practical value in modifying the views of our people in regard to the Negro Problem." He was "particularly anxious to bring home to the American people the fact that the African race in its own continent has achieved advancements which have been of importance in the development of civilization of the human race," and he wanted to "talk over the possibilities of practical steps in this direction." Washington did not respond to this letter but did extend an invitation to Boas on June 17, 1912, to serve on the executive committee of the International Conference on the Negro.[33]

There are clear indications that Boas modified Washington's image of Africans, through the influences of his ghostwriters. As early as the winter of 1903–4, Washington had begun writing a two-volume history of the Negro in Africa and America; in 1906, he assigned the writing of to Robert Ezra Park. When work of higher priority flooded Park's desk, it was put aside. Two years later, at the insistence of the publisher, the assignment went to Alvis Octavious Stafford, a teacher at the Institute for Colored Youth in Cheyney, Pennsylvania. But the drafts Stafford sent back were so poor that Monroe Nathan Work, Tuskegee's new director of Records and Research, was called in to salvage the project.[34] Writing to Washington concerning Work's contribution to the project, Park stated:

> I think I ought, now as "The Story of the Negro" is off our hands, to say something of the way in which Mr. Work has helped me during this long, tedious, and often very discouraging task. From the very first, although the work I was doing was not anything he felt responsible for and although the demands I made upon him often interfered with his own work, he has never shirked or complained. He has met every demand I made upon him in perfect cheerfulness, and has done the work I asked him to do, as faithfully as if he were working at some task of his own choosing, and according to his own methods and ideas.[35]

It was not only his diligence but his background that enabled Work to play such a monumental role in writing *The Story of the Negro*, a work—to use Harlan's words—"significant for its consciousness of Africa."[36] In 1908, Work told the story of Washington's invitation to come to Tuskegee as follows:

> Mr. Washington wrote to me and said he wanted to establish a department of history at Tuskegee in which there would be an opportunity for the study of the Negro. He had been urged to have a study made of graduates of Tuskegee. He wrote me that he wanted to see me and said that he was coming through Savannah. He was in his private car going

to Beaufort, South Carolina to make a speech. I met him and said to him, "I have your letter." He said, "Yes, come over to Tuskegee and we'll talk it over." The conversation was just a minute and didn't consume as much time as it takes me to tell you about it.[37]

In "An Autobiographical Sketch" written in 1940, however, Work portrayed himself as taking a more assertive role in the negotiations. When Washington asked him "to establish a department of Negro history," Work indicated that in his opinion "it would be more important and valuable to have a department specializing in the compiling of current data relating to the Negro. My suggestion was accepted and at Tuskegee Institute was established the first department, in a Negro Educational Institution, devoted to compiling from all available sources data relating to every phase of Negro life and history."[38]

Work added that when he came to Tuskegee, many persons who were involved in black uplift were asking questions such as "What has the Negro accomplished? What can he do? Does it pay to educate him? Morally and physically, is he not deteriorating? Has his emancipation been justified?" He noted that Frederick Hoffman's *Race Traits and Tendencies of the Negro* (1896) "had presented a more or less hopeless view" and that "to the indictment by this publication there was at hand no effective answer." Work, a person who believed that all generalizations about blacks should be based on concrete, universally verifiable data ("You can't argue with facts," he said), from 1908 on "was compiling a day by day record of what was taking place with reference to the Negro," and "thus it became possible," he believed, "to answer in a factual manner questions relating to all matters concerning him [the Negro]."[39] As a result of being asked such questions, Work began to publish the *Negro Yearbook* (a biennial) which had a worldwide circulation and became "a standard reference on all matters pertaining to the Race."[40]

Work's fascination with Africa had begun in graduate school while he was studying under William I. Thomas—a scholar influenced significantly by Franz Boas. Before the publication of *The Story of the Negro* in 1909, Work had published three articles treating Africans in the *Southern Workman*. Furthermore, in *The Story*, Work quoted Boas extensively on the art of smelting ores by Africans, the artistic industries of Africa, the agriculture of Africans, native African culture, African law, and the character of African states.[41] In sum, Work, who would later become a distinguished Africanist, was the conduit between Boasian anthropology and Washington and his other colleagues.

Robert E. Park, who had helped to ghostwrite the early chapters of *The Story*, was born on February 14, 1864, on a farm six miles from Schickshinny, Luzerene County, Pennsylvania. His mother, Theodosia Warner, was a schoolteacher; his father, Hiram Asa Park, was a soldier in the Union Army. After the Civil War the elder Park moved his family to Red Wing, Minnesota, a town located on the Mississippi River forty miles south of Minneapolis, where he established a wholesale grocery. Park spent eighteen years in Red Wing, whose population was composed mainly of Norwegian and Swedish immigrants. After graduating from high school in 1882, the young Park attended the University of Minnesota for one year before transferring to the University of Michigan, where he achieved a Ph.D. in philology in 1887.[42]

From 1887 to 1898 Park worked for various newspapers in the Midwest and New York City; attempted (unsuccessfully) to publish a novel; tried (again unsuccessfully) to publish a new type of newspaper with Franklin Ford and John Dewey, his undergraduate professor in philosophy, who, along with the Germanist Calvin Thomas had influenced him significantly during his college years. In 1894, Park married Clara Cahill, the daughter of a Michigan state supreme court justice. In 1898 he entered Harvard, intending to earn a master's degree in philosophy. Studying under William James, George Santayana, and Hugo Münsterberg, Park was, as his biographer Fred H. Matthews has pointed out, "particularly impressed by William James," who "turned him away from philosophy. He reinforced not only Park's distaste for reductionist science, but more broadly his revulsion from all abstract, categorizing thought."[43] As a consequence, in 1899 Park moved his family to Berlin, where he entered Friedrich Wilhelm University and studied under Georg Simmel, whom he later referred to as "the greatest of all sociologists." Later, under the direction of Wilhelm Windelband, he wrote his dissertation, "Masse und Publikum: Eine methodologishe und sociologische Untersuchung," at the University of Heidelberg and was awarded the doctorate in 1903.

Park returned to the United States in 1903 and worked as an assistant to William James at Harvard. In 1904 he became the secretary of the Congo Reform Association—an organization dedicated to protesting the atrocities perpetrated against the indigenous population in Belgian King Leopold's Congo Free State—and organized the American chapter through the Massachusetts Commission of Justice. Between 1904 and 1907 Park wrote four articles on the Congo which appeared in *Outlook*, *World To-Day*, and *Everybody's Magazine*. In these articles, as Stanford Lyman pointed out in 1992, Park made a transition from "Germanic romantic philosophy" toward "the rational and excessively positivistic social science that is represented today by its mainstream professional."[44]

Disillusioned with the reformers with whom he had come in contact in the Congo Reform Association, Park left that organization in 1905. He was preparing to go to Africa to study the Congo situation firsthand when he met Booker T. Washington, who suggested that he should "visit Tuskegee and start his studies of Africa in the southern states." Park, who was financially insecure, accepted Washington's offer to become press secretary for Tuskegee Institute at a salary of $150 per month, "with traveling expenses (railway fare and sleeping car, but not hotel)." In return, Park pledged that "all that I earn by writing or any other means whatever, whether more or less than $1,800 per year, unless by special arrangement, shall be either turned over to the funds of the school or charged against the $150 per month guaranteed me in this agreement."[45]

Although it was not a financially profitable position, Park later wrote: "I probably learned more about human nature and society in the South under Booker Washington than I learned elsewhere in my previous years."[46] Most significantly, in addition to *The Story of the Negro* (with Monroe N. Work), he wrote *My Larger Education* (1911) and collaborated with Washington in writing *The Man Farthest Down* (1912). At the end of his tenure at Tuskegee he told Washington: "I have never been so happy in my life as I have since I have been associated with you in this work. Some of the best friends I have in the world are at Tuskegee. I feel and shall always feel that I belong in a sort of way to the Negro race and shall continue to share, through good and evil, all its joys and sorrows. I want to help you in the future as in the past in any way I can."[47]

Nonetheless, after surveying Park's writings during his Congo Reform Association and Tuskegee Institute period, the sociologist John H. Stanfield wrote that "although Park was very aware and concerned about exploitation and control of indigenous African peoples by Europeans, this concern was transformed into an apologetic position when the issue was African Americans in the South." Furthermore, Stanfield states correctly that "although Park described at length the adaptive function of Tuskegee and similar institutions in developing the black masses, he was silent about how the model could be applied in Africa without inflicting the very kind of imposition of control he criticized."[48]

While he was working on *The Story*, Park, the radical reformer, wrote to Washington:

> As introduction on to chapter second I wish you would dictate something about your acquaintance with Africa through books and through persons.
> What was the first book aside from a geography you read about Africa or any one who had come from Africa?
> Did you ever discover when you were young any one of the books, written before the war, to prove the abilities of the Native African? If so, what impression did they make on you?

What Africans have you known[?] Have you met Dube? Did you know Dr. Edward W. Blyden?

Any personal reminiscences you can give me of these men or anything that connects you directly or indirectly with Africa I can use in the second chapter.

Do you know any of the Liberian people?

Please let me have whatever you can along this line as soon as possible.

I got a good story from the Fayette Silk Mills, though we ought to see the proprietor, who is in New York before we write anything.

I am very truly Robert E. Park.

P.S. Don't you know of some colored man who went out to Africa with high hope of settling there, or of reforming and civilizing the natives and who returned, disenchanted?[49]

Washington's response to Park's questions resulted in the appearance of the following passage in the first volume of *The Story of the Negro*:

What I was first able to hear and to learn did not, I confess, take me very far or give me very much satisfaction. In the part of the country in which I lived there were very few of my people who pretended to know very much about Africa. I learned, however, that my mother's people had come, like the white people, from across the water, but from a more distant and more mysterious land, where people lived a different life from ours, had different customs and spoke a different language from that I had learned to speak. Of the long and terrible journey by which my ancestors came from their native home in Africa to take up their life again beside the white man and Indian in the New World, I used to hear many and sinister references, but not until I was a man did I meet any one, among my people, who knew anything definite, either through personal knowledge or through tradition, of the country or the people from whom my people sprang. To most of the slaves the "middle passage," as the journey from the shore of Africa to the shore of America was called, was merely a tradition of a confused and bewildering experience concerning whose horrors they had never heard any definite details. Nothing but the vaguest notions remained, at the time I was a boy, even among the older people in regard to the mother country of my race. . . .

After I began to go to school I had my first opportunity to learn from books something further and more definite about my race in Africa. I cannot say that I received very much encouragement or inspiration from what I learned in this way while I was in school. The books I read told me of a people who roamed naked through the forest like wild beasts, of a people without houses or laws, without chastity or morality, with no family life and fixed habits of industry.

It seems to me now, as I recall my first definite impressions of my race in Africa, that the books I read when I was a boy always put the picture of Africa and African life in an unnecessarily cruel contrast with the pictures of the civilized and highly cultured Europeans and Americans. . . . In order to put the lofty position to which the white race has attained in sharper contrast with the lowly condition of a more primitive people, the best among the white people, was contrasted with the worst among the black.[50]

Washington also mentioned reading Henry Barth's *Discoveries in North and Central Africa* (1850) in reference to the "intermingling of racial stocks" in Africa.

In response to Park's question concerning the Africans he knew, the Wizard named some "pure blood" students who had received honors at Tuskegee and prominent "pure" black African Americans such as J.C. Price, Isaiah T. Montgomery, Charles Banks, W.W. Brown, Major R.R. Moten, and Paul Lawrence Dunbar. He then proceeded to tell the story of a Tuskegee student who was part Bushman and part Hottentot who talked about his people and even showed pictures demonstrating that they were "the victims of circumstances."[51] The last of Park's questions were not answered in *The Story*.

In 1909, Washington's conception of Africa changed once again when he corresponded with James H. Breasted, the Egyptologist, who taught at the University of Chicago. Breasted had been born into a Congregationalist family in 1865 in Rockford, Illinois. He had graduated from Northwestern (now North Central) College in Naperville, Illinois, attended Chicago Theological Seminary and Yale University, and received the M.A. and Ph.D. in Egyptology from the University of Berlin in 1894. The nation's leading Egyptologist believed that Ethiopia, "long supposed to have been the source of Egyptian art and civilization, actually received its culture from the Egyptians."[52] Nevertheless, he wrote to Washington on April 29, 1909:

Since 1905 I have carried out an expedition on the upper, or Nubian Nile which has brought back for the first time, exhaustive copies of all the historical monuments now surviving in that distant country. At the same time the recent discovery of papyrus documents containing translations of the New Testament into the ancient Nubian tongue is enabling us to decipher the hitherto undeciphered inscriptions of the early Nubians. The importance of all this is chiefly: that from these documents when deciphered, we shall be able to put together the only surviving information on the early history of a dark race. Nowhere else in all the world is the early history of a dark race preserved.[53]

Washington replied to Breasted on May 6 with the astute comment:

> I have noticed one fact . . . which lends a special interest to your dis-
> coveries: This is that the traditions of most of the peoples whom I have
> read, point to a distant place in the direction of ancient Ethiopia as the
> source from which [African people] received what civilization they still
> possess. This is true, I think, of the people of the Western Sudan and
> equally true of the Lake Regions.
>
> Could it be possible that these civilizing influences had their
> sources in this ancient kingdom to which your article refers?[54]

In short, by 1909 Washington's position had moved through three stages.
Influenced by nineteenth-century racist conceptions of Africans through-
out his childhood and most of his adult life, he initially conceived of his
African ancestors as primitive barbarians. As he became more involved in
African affairs and came under the influence of Work, Boas, and Park,
Washington modified his position to acknowledge the contribution of
Africans to world civilization. And finally, influenced by James H. Breasted,
he had come to the position taken by nineteenth-century African American
nationalists: that Ethiopia was the disseminator of knowledge to West
Africa. As a result, in his last address before the American Missionary
Association in 1915, Washington abandoned his earlier notions about
persons of African descent and replaced them with the idea of African
Americans as normal human stock. "There is sometimes much talk about
the inferiority of the Negro," he stated, but in practice "the idea appears to
be that he is a sort of superman. He is expected with about one fifth of
what whites received for their education to make as much progress as they
are making."[55]

4

W.E.B. Du Bois, George W. Ellis, and the Reconstruction of the Image of Africa

To a left-of-center scholar and activist like W.E.B. Du Bois, Boas's insights into the glories of the African past assumed a degree of potency that resulted in a life-long attempt to counter the right-of-center's myth of African inferiority. Even for the gifted and perceptive Du Bois, however, the process of dignifying the African past of African Americans was slow and protracted. In each of his three books on African history, written between 1915 and 1946, he was compelled to admit that he still labored

> under the difficulty of the persistent lack of interest in Africa so long characteristic of modern history and sociology. The careful, detailed researches into the history of the Negroid peoples have only begun, and the need for them is not yet clear to the thinking world. I feel compelled nevertheless to go ahead with my interpretation, even though that interpretation has here and there but slender historical proof. I believe that in the main my story is true, despite the fact that so often between the American Civil War and World War I the weight of history and science supports me only in part and in some cases appears violently to contradict me.[1]

Nonetheless, by 1946 Du Bois had made great strides in resolving the paradox that resulted from the tensions between social science and mysticism in his earlier work. In 1940 at the age of seventy-two, while tracing his "racial history" in *Dusk of Dawn: An Essay Toward an Autobiography of a Race Concept,* he recalled that during his youth he had had "only one direct cultural connection [with Africa] and that was the African melody which my great-grandmother Violet used to sing." Where she had learned it he did not know: "Perhaps she herself was born in Africa or had it of a mother or father stolen and transported." Du Bois also recognized that his mother's people's cultural patterns "were not African so much as Dutch and New England. The speech was an idiomatic New England tongue with no African dialect; the family customs were New England, and the sex mores." Thus Du Bois's "African racial feeling" was "purely a matter of my own later learning and reaction; my recoil from the assumptions of the whites;

my experience in the South at Fisk." Yet although he had obtained his "African racial feeling late in life," Du Bois thought that "it was nonetheless real and a large determinant of life and character. . . . I felt myself African by `race,' and by that token was African and an integral member of the group of dark Americans who were called Negroes."[2]

In the first Atlanta University publication he edited, *Some Efforts of American Negroes for Their Own Social Betterment* (1898), Du Bois referred to African religion as the "mystery and rites of . . . fetishism." Despite this stereotype, he anticipated Melville J. Herskovits's work on African retentions in *The Myth of the Negro Past* (1941) when he wrote: "The Negro Church is the only social institution of Negroes which started in the African forest and survived slavery; under the leadership of the priest and medicine man, . . . the Church preserved in itself the remnants of African tribal life."[3] How did Du Bois know the Negro Church started in the "African forest," or that it was a custodian of "African tribal life"? He did not footnote these statements, nor had he done fieldwork in Africa. It is somewhat ironic that the author of the 1898 article "The Study of Negro Problems," which had accused white commentators on "the Negro Problem" of lacking a "deep sense of the sanctity of scientific truth," was guilty of a similar failing.[4] Furthermore, Du Bois made such undocumented statements as "There are undoubted proofs that the native Africans, or at least most Negro tribes, are born merchants and traffickers and drive good bargains even with Europeans"; and again in 1899 in *The Negro in Business*, "The African Negro is a born trader." He was correct in his assertion that in the "communism of the slave plantation considerable barter went on among the slaves, and between them and whites," but whether or not this was an African tradition is another matter.[5]

Du Bois had of course heard Boas speak about African history at Atlanta University in 1906.[6] Du Bois later told Harold R. Isaacs: "I did not myself begin actively to study Africa until 1908 or 1910. Franz Boas really influenced me to begin studying this subject and I began really to get into it only after 1915."[7] It was perhaps due to his relationship with Boas that Du Bois tried to rationalize his attempt to "connect present conditions with the African past." He had made that effort, he declared in *The Negro American Family* (1908),

> not because Negro-Americans are Africans, or can trace an unbroken social history from Africa, but because there is a distinct nexus between Africa and America which, though broken and perverted, is nevertheless not to be neglected by the careful student. It is, however, exceedingly difficult and puzzling to know just where to find the broken thread of African and American social history. Accurate scientific inquiry must trace the social history in the seventeenth and eight-

eenth centuries of such Negro tribes as furnished material for the American slave trade. This inquiry is unfortunately impossible. We do not know accurately which tribes are represented in America, and we have but chance pictures of Negro social conditions in those times. Assuming, however, that the condition of Negro tribes in the nineteenth century reflected much of their earlier conditions, and that central and west Africa furnished most of the slaves, some attempt has been made to picture in broad outline the social evolution of the Negro in his family relations.[8]

Du Bois tended to push Boas's claim for the glorious African past to its furthest limits. In *Efforts for Social Betterment among Negro Americans* (1909), he asserted: "If there is one thing in which the life of [African] barbarians shows a decided superiority to that of civilized people it is in the solution to the problem of poverty. . . . There was no need [for charity] among Africans, since all shared the common fund of land and food."[9] By 1914, in *Morals and Manners among Negro Americans*, Du Bois was even more aggressively inventing traditions:

> Africa is distinctly the land of the Mother. In subtle and mysterious ways, despite her curious history, her slavery, polygamy and toil, the spell of the African mother pervades her land. Isis, the Mother, is still titular goddess in thought, if not in name, of the dark continent. This does not seem to be solely a survival of the historic matriarchy through which all nations pass. It appears to be more than this, as if the black race in passing down the steps of human culture gave the world not only the Iron Age, the cultivation of the soil and the domestication of animals but also in peculiar emphasis the Mother-idea.[10]

In 1915, Du Bois published *The Negro*, a slim volume which traced the history of Africans and African Americans from the rise of Egypt to Du Bois's own day. It was not intended to be a thorough treatment of a subject on which there were few reliable historical data, nor was it intended to be merely an addition to the historical knowledge of the period. It was written to inform the public so that policy decisions in regard to blacks in both Africa and the Americas would be unbiased. Given the endemic racism of the period, "one who writes of the development of the Negro race must continually insist that he is writing of a normal human stock, and that whatever it is fair to predicate of the mass of human beings may be predicated of the Negro. It is the silent refusal to do this which has led to so much false writing on Africa."[11]

The Negro was a tale told to discredit the white supremacists' "assumption . . . that color is a mark of inferiority." Du Bois first refuted the contemporaneous definition of race: "To-day no scientific definition of race is possible. Differences, and striking differences, there are between men and groups of men, but they fade into each other so insensibly that we can only indicate the main divisions of men in broad outlines." He concluded this section by stating that he was "studying the history of the darker part of the human family, which is separated from the rest of mankind by no absolute physical line, but which nevertheless forms, as a mass, a social group distinct in history, appearance, and to some extent in spiritual gift."[12]

Du Bois refuted the contention of George R. Gliddon and Josiah Nott—both members of the proslavery American school of ethnology—who, on the basis of Egyptian material culture, claimed to have demonstrated that Negroes had served only as slaves in Egypt. Du Bois argued that the dynasty which began with Aha-Mena in 4777 B.C. had "many Pharaohs . . . of a strongly Negroid cast of countenance," and that "Egypt was herself always palpably Negroid, and from her vantage ground as almost the only African gateway received and transmitted Negro ideals." Furthermore, he took to task contemporaneous Egyptologists such as James H. Breasted, who had concluded that Ethiopia was not the "source of Egyptian art and civilization." "The Egyptians themselves," Du Bois asserted, "in later days, affirmed that they and their civilization came from the south and from the black tribes of Punt."[13]

Like Breasted, Du Bois was a diffusionist, but unlike Breasted, he believed that from Ethiopia "the black originators of African culture, and to a large degree world culture, wandered not simply down the Nile, but also westward." Ethiopians, he said, "developed the original substratum of culture which later influences modified but never displaced." To undermine the belief that the indigenous peoples of the Sudan had made no original contributions to the civilizations of those regions, Du Bois declared:

> We know the Egyptian Pharaohs in several cases ventured into the western Sudan and that Egyptian influences are distinctly traceable. Greek and Byzantine culture and Phoenician and Carthaginian trade also penetrated, while Islam finally made this whole land her own. Behind all these influences, however, stood from the first an indigenous Negro culture. The stone figures of Sherbro, the megaliths of Gambia, the art and industry of the west coast are all too deep and original evidences of civilization to be merely importations from abroad.[14]

In tracing the history of Ghana, Mali, Songhay, and other ancient kingdoms of the Sudan, Du Bois stated unequivocally: "Islam did not found new states, but modified and united Negro states already ancient; it did not initiate new commerce but developed a widespread trade already established." He closed the chapter with a polemical statement: "It is a curious commentary on modern prejudice that most of this splendid history of civilization and uplift is unknown to-day, and men confidently assert that Negroes have no history."[15]

August Meier has written that in Du Bois's first book on Africa he "brought to bear . . . not only the historical knowledge then available, but also the latest anthropological studies, including the work of Franz Boas." The work "was notable for its extensive, sophisticated discussion of the history and cultures of Africa south of the Sahara. . . . [It] attested to the crystallization of black history as a research specialty."[16] Meier could have noted also that Du Bois was taking part in the revolt against formalism and thereby helping to revolutionize the historical profession in the United States.

The "new history" had its origins in 1907, when James Harvey Robinson and Charles A. Beard published *The Development of Modern Europe*. Rebelling against the "scientific history" of Leopold von Ranke, which attempted to describe things as they really happened and focused on political history, Beard and Robinson suggested that history should interpret or explain all kinds of social facts, and that explanations or interpretations were to be established according to the canons of all reliable knowledge. Du Bois embraced this emphasis on historicism (defined by Morton White as "the attempt to explain facts by reference to earlier facts") and cultural organicism (defined by White as "the attempt to find explanations and relevant material in social sciences other than the one which is primarily under investigation").[17]

Du Bois's enthusiasm for historicism is obvious in the following passage:

> At first sight it would seem that slavery completely destroyed every vestige of spontaneous movement among the Negroes. This is not strictly true. The vast power of the priest in the African state is well known; his realm alone—the province of religion and medicine—remained largely unaffected by the plantation system. The Negro priest, therefore, early became an important figure on the plantation and found his function as the interpreter of the supernatural, the comforter of the sorrowing, and as the one who expressed, rudely but picturesquely, the longing and disappointment and resentment of a stolen people. From such beginnings arose and spread with marvelous rapidity the Negro Church, the first distinctively Negro American social institution. It was not at first by any means a Christian church, but a mere adaptation of those rites of fetish which in America is termed worship or voodooism. . . . It is historic fact, that the Negro church of today bases itself upon the sole surviving social institution of the African fatherland, that accounts for its extraordinary growth and vitality.[18]

In short, the historical validation for the hypothesis concerning African retentions which was later adopted by Melville J. Herskovits, whose impact on African and African American studies is potent to this day, had its origins in the revolt against formalism. In embracing cultural organicism as well, Du Bois drew from the new social science methodology, from new scientific investigations of African culture, and from new cultural anthropological investigations of blacks. His attempt to seek "explanations and relevant material" in anthropology is reflected in Clark Wissler's letter of December 7, 1909, responding to Du Bois's inquiry about "a list of the best works on Negro anthropology and ethnology." Wissler, a disciple of Boas, wrote: "The fact is that the literature upon this subject is very incomplete and unsatisfactory. The best brief article, with which I am acquainted will be found in the History of Mankind by Ratzel. There is a small book by Deniker on the Races of Man, Scribners. In the footnotes to the discussion of Africa you will find references to all the important literature of the subject, and while this book is brief, it is in some respects a digest of our present knowledge."[19]

Du Bois did not rely on either Friedrich Ratzel or Joseph Deniker in his discussions of racial differences and the origin and characteristics of blacks when he published *The Negro* in 1915. By the time that book was published, he had found the works of Boas, Sergi, Ernst Loeb, William Z. Ripley, and Jean Finot more in line with his ideology. In 1987 St. Clair Drake showed that Du Bois's investigation into the "Classical Greco-Roman sources and material published by Egyptologists" resulted in the demolition of the thesis held by ethnologists (Nott and Gliddon) and contemporaneous Egyptologists (James Breasted, William M.F. Petrie, Gustav Maspero, E.A. Wallis Budge, Percy E. Newberry, John Garstang) that the "Egyptians were *dark-skinned Caucasians* descended from Noah's son Ham." Du Bois's position had, in short, evolved from one that stressed African primitivism to one that was, in Drake's words, "surprisingly close to that of contemporary [late twentieth-century] mainstream Egyptology."[20]

Like W.E.B. Du Bois, George W. Ellis attempted, after a brief spell of stereotyping Africans, to reconstruct their image. After only three years in Liberia, Ellis had espoused an anthropogeographical determinist position, believing, like Joseph A. Tillighast, that, "tropical nature is wont to sustain the idle and the indolent without the dint of labor." Then, assuming, as most of the proponents of neo-Lamarckianism did, that a group's aptitude for achievement was directly affected by the physical environment, Ellis wrote: "The natural effect of climatic conditions is to impair one's desire and ability for intellectual and physical labor." Although he admitted that some of the tribes of Liberia "have men possessed of great knowledge concerning the medicinal qualities of plants, herbs, and roots," and that "the industrial products of the Mandingoes represent a varied use of natural resources and indicate a high order of industrial skill," he nevertheless believed that there were differences in the aptitudes of the various ethnic groups of Liberia. In other words, like white racists, Ellis subordinated individual differences to group differences. "All these tribes," he wrote, possess "different degrees of natural capacity."[21]

On April 4, 1906, writing to Otis T. Mason, the head curator of the National Museum in Washington, D.C., Ellis still drew crude distinctions between African ethnic groups, mentioning that he found himself "amid a group of peoples of *varied grades of primitive culture* [emphasis added]." In passing, he stated that he wanted "to try to compare the Vais with the Gora or Gola-speaking Peoples, a very powerful and warlike people with four tribal varieties."[22]

Perhaps Ellis would have continued to indulge in such stereotypical thinking had it not been for the 1907 article by Franz Uri Boas titled "The Anthropological Position of the Negro," published in the *Van Norden Magazine* in April. After reading it, Ellis wrote Boas on May 28:

> To my mind you have stated fairly the position of science as to the ascertained inferiority of Negro peoples and to my mind struck at the very foundation of those erroneous opinions so widely diffused among Caucasian nations, founded upon the supposed conclusions of science, and which have entailed so much injury and injustice upon the darker races. It is a great tribute to any man to announce the truth, but it is a greater tribute to send it forth into a hostile world, when the author must know that it will be received with disfavor and derision by so many millions of his race. But the circle of those who adhere to your views slowly but constantly widens with the processes of the suns.[23]

Ellis asked Boas in this same letter to refer him to a publisher or a magazine that might be interested in his manuscript on the Vai tribes of West Africa, whom he had just spent six months observing.

Boas, who did not receive Ellis's missive until he returned to New York City from Europe in August, replied on August 28 that he was "very much interested in" what Ellis said and would "be very glad if I can help you in the publication of your observations on the natives of West Africa." He cautioned Ellis, however, that it was "not quite easy . . . to get material of this kind published . . . If you should care to send me a chapter as a sample, I could tell you more definitely what can be done."[24]

The outcome of Boas's efforts to get Ellis published is unknown, but on July 15, 1908, Ellis told W.E.B. Du Bois, whom he had met on January

1, 1906, at the African Methodist Church in Washington, D.C., that he had "secured 100 folklore stories and 150 proverbs and prepared a MS of 60,000 words for press in London, Harrison & Sons." He indicated to Du Bois that he was going to visit the "Vai country" during the dry season in order to take "100 pictures of scenes in actual life" as visual material for the manuscript. His intention at this juncture was to test Jerome Dowd's contention in *The Negro Races* (1907) "that the study of the Negro Question in America should be begun in America." Ellis admitted to Du Bois that he would "not express any opinion as to the correctness of this view"; he only wished to say that he found the "study interesting" and wished that he "had the time, talent and money to work up [his] subject as it should be."[25]

What happened to Ellis's negotiations with Harrison and Sons is not known, but we do know that after he returned to the United States and a lucrative legal practice in southside Chicago, he began negotiations in December 1912 with the Neale Publishing Company in New York City for the publication of the manuscript on the Vai peoples. After extensive negotiations, Neale brought out Ellis's book, *Negro Culture in West Africa*, in November 1914.[26] The intention of this monumental work was not only to discredit the previous scholarship of social scientists such as Joseph A. Tillinghast and Jerome Dowd, and the contemporary works of "social gospel prophets" such as James Shepard Dennis, Robert Elliott Speer, Arthur Tappan Pierson, and Frederic Perry Noble, but also to replace their racist mythology with an ecumenical one.

At the outset Ellis informed his readers that one of his purposes was to help clarify the American race issue—primarily because "the interracial understanding between what is considered the two most divergent and dissimilar ethnic groups" was "largely conditioned upon knowledge possessed of the Negro in Africa." He astutely pointed out that much of the information he had found in encyclopedias, geographies, and works of ethnologists and anthropologists before he went to Liberia was later "disclosed to be unsupported by the facts." It was not that this image of the Negro in Africa had been intentionally concocted, Ellis argued, but that "science had hitherto in the main been compelled to rely upon the reports and data supplied by transient travellers and resident visitors who little understood African mentality, institutions and society." To be sure, when the European nations partitioned Africa, a group of administrators and "capable resident students"—persons such as Sir Harry H. Johnston, Sir A.B. Ellis, Mary H. Kingsley, Lady Lugard, Dr. J. Scott Keltie, Count de Cardi, E.D. Morel, M. Felix Du Bois, and Dr. Robert H. Nassau—began to present a more realistic depiction of the sub-Saharan African. Nevertheless, Ellis thought it "necessary and imperative . . . that the Negro should explain his own culture and interpret his own thought and soul life . . . if the complete truth is to be given to the other races of the earth." In writing Negro Culture in West Africa, Ellis felt that he was contributing "his proper portion toward the ultimate concord and cooperation of the races in the great upward trend of social progress."[27]

First, the book took to task those commentators such as the Wesleyan Academy—trained Vai prince, Thomas E. Beselow, who argued that Vais were of Abyssinian origin. On the basis of the best evidence he could gather, Ellis concurred in Rev. S.W. Koelle's theory that the Vai people belonged "to the Mande branch of the Negro race," which had "been affected by the same forces that influenced the great Negroland from without and . . . they originated from the Mandingoes in the Hinterland of Liberia." Second, to counter the myth that the majority of Africans could be represented by what ethnologists had described as the "Negro type," Ellis pointed out that "in personal features . . . the great majority of Vais afford a flat contradiction to the generally accepted Negro type, although they live under climatic conditions characterized by the most severe and deteriorating influences." Third, Ellis discredited the myth that because West Africa's climate provided such abundant food, the inhabitants were not forced to spend much time cultivating the soil or to develop a high degree of "industrial efficiency." From his firsthand observation of the Vai people, Ellis concluded that their economic life, "far from being dependent upon natural products, includes cultivation of food materials, the sale of imported articles as well as of the products of their own industrial skill."[28]

In order to refute Tillinghast's contention that West Africans did not inhibit their "sexual proclivities and neglected their youth," Ellis demonstrated that "the Vais live in social groups necessitated by physical conditions, and they maintain their various secret societies as means by which individuals are governed and prepared for native life. Witchcraft and the social dance are important factors in Vai life." Furthermore, Ellis denied that African blacks were incapable of abstraction: "In fundamentals the Vai language discloses its relationship to the great languages of the world and it is rich and musical in the concords of its sounds. . . . The written Vai language," he added somewhat chauvinistically, "[is] a great invention of the Negro brain, original in conception and independent in character."[29]

Ellis saved his most damning criticisms of white commentators for the social gospel prophets who depicted sub-Saharan Africa—to use Ralph E. Luker's words—as the locus of "appalling social conditions among Africa's people." It was purportedly a place in which Islam and Christianity vied for the soul of pagan, indolent, and morally debased Africans who reveled in deceit and savagery. And proponents of the social gospel, though critical of "imperialist greed," nevertheless sought to replicate "American Christendom" by sending African American missionaries to Africa.[30]

Ellis was especially critical of Frederic Perry Noble's assertion in *The Redemption of Africa* that "the Negro is unmoral." After surveying the literature "by competent minds . . . conversant with the dialects and languages of the localities being studied"—Mary H. Kingsley, A.B. Ellis, M. le Comte de Cardi, E.D. Morel, T.J. Alldridge, C.B. Wallis, John Hardford, Caseley Hayford, John Sarbah, and Edward Wilmot Blyden—Ellis concluded: "The quotations from the authorities now extant on the Negro and his life showing that he has not only moral conceptions but moral standards would make a volume."[31]

Yet Ellis was not a moral relativist. He still carried much of the nineteenth-century African American "civilizationist" ideology intact, for like Alexander Crummell he was a staunch advocate of the three Cs—Civilization, Christianity, and Commerce—as the most efficient means of redeeming Africa.[32] According to Ellis, the Vai culture was divided into two elements: the native and the Islamic. The pagan religious life and practice of the Vais, he believed, had certain defects—that is, "superstitions and mysteries"—but their paganism was "still the means" by which they had "sought to find and serve their God." Although respectful of the Vais' form of pantheism, Ellis nevertheless saw Islam, to which he thought some 60 percent of the Vais adhered as "a vital, living, active force" that stirred "the spiritual nature . . . to its very depths." Ellis believed those Vais "who profess the faith of the Meccan prophet evince a superiority over their pagan tribesman and possess a zeal, dignity, and devotion which at least are impressive."[33]

Revealing the racialist deterministic thinking that was endemic to African American thought, Ellis argued that the primary appeal for the Vais of the Islamic faith was the teaching that "the Negro has an honorable part in the military history and noted achievements of the religion."[34]

> By the best informed Muhummadans the Africans are made to feel a pride in the fact that their race is recognized in the Koran, which contains a chapter inscribed to a Negro, and that Muhammud was in part descended from an African and had a Negro as a confidant in Arabia. It is pointed out that Negroes figured prominently in the progress of Islam, and on one occasion slew a rival of Muhhamud. It is said that the prophet greatly admired a Negro poet of ant[e]-Islamic times, and regretted that he had never seen him.[35]

Yet for Ellis, Christianity was far superior to all other religions. As early as December 8, 1909, speaking at the Protestant Episcopal church in Monrovia, Liberia, he argued that "no state has ever been able to rise above the conception and character of its god" and stated: "Christianity unified . . . two hostile elements, harmonized the freedom of the North with the culture of the South, and started modern Europe upon the construction of the most progressive, the most powerful and the most imposing civilization which has ever attracted the attention and thought of the human race." Thus, "on account of its universal adaptability, its many sidedness, and its all-embracing truth, Christianity is the great religion of the world."[36] Even though most of the Vais were either pagans or Moslems, Ellis believed that Christianity—first introduced to them by an Americo-Liberian, Rev. Daniel Ware, in 1860—was slowly taking hold. After assessing the efforts of Christian educators and missionaries among the Vai-speaking people, Ellis concluded: "Science, literature, art, philosophy, and Christianity will do for the Vais what they have done for the nations—that is, enable them to utilize their natural resources and actualize their highest social and spiritual destiny." Once "Christianity and Modern Civilization" were given "Vai roots," he said, "the Crescent [Islam]" would "wane before the Cross."[37]

Ellis attributed the Crescent's previous victories over the Cross to three Vai objections to the latter: "its disintegrating influences upon the family and the state, . . . caste distinctions based on race, and . . . the liquor traffic carried on by individuals living among Christian nations." Commenting on the first of these, Ellis admitted that Christianity might "tend to disintegrate the Negro family, founded upon polygamy," but still believed that Christianity "in the truest and best sense . . . is a great integrating and socializing factor among peoples who are prepared to understand and practice Christian principles, and who have not the weaknesses and the prejudices of undeveloped minds." For him, polygamy was "inconsistent with the highest social and spiritual development of mankind," but he recommended that "the destruction of polygamy in Africa be accompanied by the modern agents for progress and development that are suitable to the peculiarities of African environment."[38]

As to the second objection, that Christianity upheld caste distinctions, "it cannot be argued that Christianity favors any such distinctions," Ellis maintained. Although the white race in South Africa and the southern states of America had "naturally confused difference with inferiority," he thought it "wise for the Negro in Africa to accept [Christian] principles and furnish the world the example of what the true Christian ought to be." He also found unreasonable the objection that some persons in Christian countries were engaged in the liquor traffic, because "there are few things so generally opposed by Christians as the liquor habit." He admitted that the "liquor traffic" was "a curse to Africa"—"just as slavery was in America"—but believed that "when Christianity and Civilization have wrought sufficient progress among the nations the liquor traffic will be stopped."[39]

Ellis was as adamant in his defense of European civilization as he was of Christianity. He agreed that the Africans in the interior, where African culture held sway, were superior to those who lived on the coast in contact with Europeans, but he held that "in all periods of transition the individual suffers but society gains." The problem was that the coastal Africans "had too much contact with the evils of civilized nations, and too little contact with their virtues." For Ellis, the assimilation of the African was the "moral obligation of civilized powers toward Africa." Yet "the power of European Civilization to actualize for the African his highest social destiny" would lead to the destruction of that power he added.[40]

Finally, Ellis smuggled in an argument for the superiority of the Negro soul and thus completed his Crummellian-Bookerite synthesis:

> The spiritual nature of the Negro has often excited comment. The meekness with which the American Negro endured the cruelties of slavery and his loyalty to the southern people during the rebellion have both been the subjects of comment. The latter has been cited to his credit and it may be that the former can be. The New Zealanders, the American Indians, the natives of Fiji and of the Sandwich Islands before the civilization of the white man have passed or are passing from the stage of action. The American Negro alone seems to increase and develop. It may be that the Negro's life and training in West Africa have been of service to him in the United States of America.[41]

Despite the enthusiasm and hard work Ellis put into the research and writing of *Negro Culture in West Africa* and the book's enthusiastic critical reception by both W.E.B. Du Bois and Robert E. Park, the work was a commercial failure, and the publisher did not hesitate to express his dissatisfaction in 1915. When the bindery was destroyed by fire in 1919, Neale wrote to cancel the contract of publication and turn over all the company's rights in the book to Ellis—but by that time the author was deceased.[42]

Two years before his death Ellis had published a poorly written novel, *The Leopard's Claw*. Replete with stereotypes of Europeans, Euro-Americans, and West Africans, it marked a retreat from his attempt at un-biased depiction of West Africans in the interior. Emphasizing fetishes, cannibalism, lying, and deceit, *The Leopard's Claw* was a portrayal of sub-Saharan Africa which resembled the myths of the social gospel prophets. The only redeeming characters of West African ancestry in the entire novel are the loyal servants of the English protagonists. Apparently, despite his previous attempts to correct the erroneous impressions of West Africa that permeated American society, in the end Ellis succumbed to the pressures of that society.

Still, although the Progressive era was one of the lowest points in the history of black-white relations in the United States, it did foster a rational, scientific approach to the problem of race relations. This approach found sufficient evidence to support the idea that African Americans were descendants of peoples who had made, and were perfectly capable of making in the present and future, achievements essential to human progress. This point of view, presented most eloquently by Franz Boas and W.E.B. Du Bois, countered the political mythology that defended the status quo. It succeeded in modifying the position of the elite defenders of the status quo, such as Booker T. Washington, whose tales about the past legitimized existing relations between blacks and whites in the early 1900s.

Thus, by 1918, when the country was undergoing tremendous economic hardships, the idea that African Americans were the descendants of barbarians who would be capable of improvement only in the distant future was being challenged. Although the myth of African inferiority remained dominant in all disciplines in "history" for many years, the first major challenge to it occurred in the monumental work of Franz Boas, who had been initially appalled by the social problems of the blacks who migrated to New York City in the 1900s. Furthermore, in the 1900s and 1910s the visibility of thousands of underclass blacks appalled many prominent sociologists and anthropologists in the cities in which they lived and worked. For historians, however, almost another forty years was necessary to extirpate the myth of African inferiority from their discipline.

5

Robert Ezra Park and American Race and Class Relations

Since the mid-1960s, sociological discussions of the present and future of racial equality in the social order of the United States have been marred by assessments that are both conflicting and controversial. The major scholarly debate centers on the question of whether the United States is progressive with respect to its black population. In 1978 William J. Wilson argued in *The Declining Significance of Race* that class rather than race was the most salient variable in race relations in contemporary America. He declared unequivocally that "race declined in importance in the economic sector" during the post–World War II period, and that the "Negro class structure became more differentiated and black life chances became more increasingly a consequence of class affiliation."[1] For Wilson, then, the question of the progressiveness of the United States is dependent chiefly upon one's unit of analysis.

Wilson's provocative arguments have generated trenchant criticism[2] but not until Alphonso Pinkney published *The Myth of Black Progress* in 1984 did Wilson's emphasis on the saliency of class undergo rigorous empirical scrutiny. Pinkney's data reveal that Wilson's formulations were premature. Although convinced that "racism was on the decline in the 1960s and 1970s," Pinkney has found scant evidence for Wilson's belief in a decline of the importance of race in the economic sector. His data indicate that the faltering United States economy during the late 1970s and early 1980s undermined earlier economic gains by blacks and distracted attention from the marginal position of blacks in the economy—an issue that had barely begun to be addressed during the late 1960s and early 1970s. On the basis of his investigation, Pinkney has concluded that "race is still the critical variable."[3]

A third, primarily theoretical perspective, which concurs in Pinkney's argument for the saliency of the race variable, was presented by Pierre van den Berghe in 1981. Van den Berghe's *The Ethnic Phenomenon* was grounded in the theories of sociobiologists. Since the work stressed the "primordial" nature of ethnic and race relations, it represented Van den Berghe's conscious attempt to bring "the beasts back in" to sociological theory. In the attempt, he constructed a pessimistic theory indicating that ethnic and racial domination will always be with us. Unlike Pinkney, Van den Berghe suggested that the condition and destiny of blacks in the United States are not amenable to political and economic solutions.[4]

The roots of the debate between Wilson and Pinkney may be found primarily, though not exclusively, in the years 1894 to 1943—from the publication of Franz Boas's "Human Faculty as Determined by Race" to the publication of Robert E. Park's in 1943. It is my argument that the parameters of the discussion of the progressiveness of race relations in the United States were defined during those years, and that all current theories are extensions of or reactions to the theories formulated during the fifty-year period that marked the formative years of American anthropology and sociology.

The current dispute among students of race relations over the greater saliency of class or race had its origins in the confrontation between nineteenth-century raciology and environmentalism in the 1890s. The idea of class differentiation within the black population emerged as a key theoretical concept in anthropology and sociology during these years, primarily because reform-minded scholars such as Franz Boas and W.E.B. Du Bois were intent on undermining the social scientific foundations of racism in their respective disciplines. In countering the stereotype of blacks as persons incapable of matching the intellectual, cultural, and economic achievements of middle-class Americans of British ancestry, they effectively challenged the racism and ethnocentrism that directly affected their lives in the cities and universities where they lived and worked.

Furthermore, between 1894 and 1943 there were several significant developments in the social science of race relations. First, from 1894 to 1911 Franz Boas attempted to free the discipline from *most* of the racial-determinist assumptions of nineteenth-century social science. The thrust of Boas's argument was that white prejudice was the major obstacle to the progress of African Americans not their assumed racial traits. As race relations changed in the North—following the Great Migration's nationalization of the "Negro problem" and the subsequent entrance of African Americans into the professions—Boas trained a group of students who were committed to what Carl N. Degler calls "the ideological principle of equality of opportunity."[5] Second, while Boas was issuing the prescriptive statement that a just society should approximate a proportional distribution of blacks and whites in all classes in the American social order, W.E.B. Du Bois was uncovering evidence that blacks were already a heterogeneous group. Du Bois, like Boas, viewed white prejudice as an obvious obstacle to black progress, but believing that historical antecedents and individual enterprise were factors to be considered, he argued that the degree of progress that some blacks were making at the turn of the century was determined by their class affiliation.

Ironically, the ideas of black progress and class differentiation within the black population served not only the ideological needs of progressives but also those of white southerners who were intent on perpetuating their region's caste-like system. Before 1915 southern whites such as Howard W. Odum argued that the existence of class differentiation among the blacks indicated the potential for a truly "separate but equal" society in the South. Visualizing what Park would later describe as a biracial organization of society, Odum concluded in *Social and Mental Traits of the Negro* (1910) that "the Negro has an unlimited field before him in the higher work of teaching, preaching, and professional work among his own people. There will be no competition there outside his own."[6] Odum's views led him to argue that blacks and whites would never mix and mingle freely—primarily because the inherent abilities of blacks rendered them incapable of competing effectively with whites, and the existence of "the mores" would prevent black-white competition.

During the 1910s and 1920s Odum's static view was modified by Robert E. Park, the erstwhile newspaper reporter and reformer. Park utilized the constellation of ideas—approximate black equality, black progress, and differentiation within the black class structure—of reform-minded social scientists (Boas, Du Bois, George E. Howard, Ellsworth Faris, Edward B. Reuter, R.R. Wright Jr., George Edmund Haynes, Monroe Nathan Work, Kelly Miller, James P. Lichtenberger, Carl Kelsey) and counterbalanced them against the ideas of an "instinctive" prejudice and William Graham Sumner's concept of "the mores" as expressed in the writings of such southern social scientists as Odum, John M. Mecklin, and Alfred Holt Stone.[7] In so doing, he constructed his own theory of a "biracial organization" of society.

Park's early theory was based on certain fundamental assumptions about the nature of race relations, assumptions that adversely affected any disposition to believe that American society was moving toward the assimilation of African Americans into the mainstream of society. His biracial organization theory was a conservative's mythical formulation of Booker T. Washington's theory of race relations within the historical context of turn-of-the-century sociology. To understand why it emerged as a rationalization for Washington's motto—"In all things that are purely social we can be as separate as the fingers, yet one as the hand in all things essential to mutual progress,"—it is necessary to analyze Park's relation to Washington, to examine his assessment of the relative capabilities of blacks and whites, and to comprehend his analysis of prejudice. Only then is it possible to understand why Park tenaciously embraced his theory in a period of inexorable change.

When Park met Booker T. Washington in 1905, the motivating force for his association with Washington was not only—as John H. Stanfield II has demonstrated—that "he agreed with the Tuskegee conception of black education and race relations, but, more importantly, [that] he needed money." Nevertheless, Park served Washington well as secretary and ghost-writer, familiarizing himself with the life histories and the statistical data on African American conditions which Washington presented to general audiences.[8] Park's own explanation of why he joined Washington was expressed in far more idealistic terms. "I was disgusted," he later recalled, "with what I had done in the University and had come to the conclusion that I couldn't do anything first rate on my own account . . . I decided the best thing to do was to attach myself to someone who was doing something first rate. Washington was not a brilliant man or an intellectual, but he seemed to me to be doing something real."[9] For his part, Washington was impressed by Park's hard work and sincerity. Although Park was a Harvard graduate, Washington indicated in 1906 that he did not know whether Park was a "graduate of any college or what college," but he considered him to be "a broad, sympathetic, strong, helpful man."[10]

Park became disillusioned with Washington when the latter espoused the belief that lower-class Europeans were worse off than African Americans, but he persisted in working with Washington even after he left Tuskegee for Chicago in 1913.[11] Having accepted William I. Thomas's invitation to join the faculty at the University of Chicago, Park taught the fall term in 1913 and added the summer term in 1914 and later years. In 1919 he was appointed professional lecturer, and finally, in 1923, he was appointed to a full professorship. He went on to train some notable students of race relations, among them E. Franklin Frazier, Horace Cayton, Charles S. Johnson, Romanzo Adams, Andrew W. Lind, Edward B. Reuter, William O. Brown, Bertram Doyle, and Louis Wirth.

During his tenure at Tuskegee, with Washington's material and moral support, Park had been able to observe the socially and economically stratified African American communities in the South. The expressed purpose of one trip was to give "Mr. Washington and his party an opportunity to see the masses of the Negro and to note their condition in all the varied circumstances which Southern life presents." Among the noteworthy persons with whom Park and Washington traveled throughout Tennessee in 1909 were William H. Lewis, assistant United States district attorney of Boston; John E. Bush, receiver of public moneys of Little Rock, Arkansas; Bishop I.B. Scott of Monrovia, Liberia, who was "in charge of the missions of the

Methodist Episcopal Church of the West Coast of Africa"; Major Robert
Russa Moton of Hampton Institute, Virginia; and J.C. Napier of Nashville,
the last African American on the Nashville city council and then cashier of
the One Cent Savings Bank, the older of the two African American banks
in Nashville. "Other members of the party," Park observed, "were bankers
and business men, teachers, preachers, all of them men who have worked
their way up to positions and influence among the colored people in their
communities."[12]

Park's account of that 1909 journey indicates the extent of his careful
observations, both of "the masses" of blacks and of the number of African
Americans who had achieved property and skills despite the caste system.

> In the eastern part of Tennessee they saw for the most part, a mining
> population in which the whites largely outnumbered the Negroes. In
> central Tennessee, in the region north of Nashville, they found a large
> population at work in the coal mines and in the tobacco fields. In the
> region around Memphis, they saw a Negro population which is com-
> posed of people who come from the cotton plantations. Memphis prob-
> ably has, at the present time, the largest Negro population in the
> United States, and Shelby County, in which Memphis is situated, prob-
> ably has the most concentrated Negro population in the United States.
> In each of the principal cities visited the party found a little group of
> prosperous Negro business men. In Chattanooga for example, two of
> the best drug stores in the city are conducted by colored men. A col-
> ored man also owns the handsome three-story brick building adjoining
> the municipal auditorium where Mr. Washington spoke . . . to an audi-
> ence of 6,000 persons.
>
> Nashville probably has the most prosperous and the most intelli-
> gent community of colored people of any city in the South. There are
> not less than six Negro business men in that city who are estimated to
> be worth at least $100,000. Nashville has also two Negro banks, and is
> the home of the National Baptist Publishing Company, which prints
> most of the literature for the million and a half colored Baptists in the
> United States. This concern publishes nine periodicals, and does an
> annual yearly business of more than $200,000.
>
> Memphis has in it R.R. Church, who is said to pay taxes on
> $220,000 worth of property, the wealthiest Negro in the state. Mr.
> Church owns, among other things, an amusement park in the center of
> the city, which contains the auditorium in which Mr. Washington
> spoke. . . . The colored people of Memphis also have one bank, a hos-
> pital and two colleges, one of them a medical school, and all of them
> supported entirely by the contributions of the Negro people in this
> vicinity.
>
> The colored people seem to be doing particularly well in the
> country districts. One of the places visited by the party was the city of

Hopkinsville, Ky., which is just over the edge of Tennessee, and the center of the Burley tobacco region. Hopkinsville was the scene a few months ago of one of the famous exploits of the Kentucky night riders. The colored tobacco farmers in this region are doing particularly well, and one of them, Tom Wright of Cerulian Springs, is said to have taken the prize regularly for a number of years for the best sample of dark tobacco produced in Christian County. Near this city, also, is the famous St. Bernard mining company's properties, where 3,600 colored and 2,000 white miners are employed. The head of this company, J.B. Atkinson, is recognized as a friend of the colored people. For example, his private secretary, bank boss in one of his mines, that is to say, the man that has charge of all the operations below ground, and a number of other men occupying responsible positions are Negroes. Mr. Atkinson employs three Negro electricians who were educated at Armour Institute, Chicago, at his expense. One of the wealthiest citizens of Hopkinsville was Peter Postelle, a colored man who died a few years ago worth $300,000.

At the meeting in Chattanooga, Mr. Washington was introduced by L.H. Coleman, a distinguished attorney of Chattanooga, who varied the usual formulas of introduction by relating to the audience facts to show to what extent the colored people have improved in Chattanooga in the 10 years since Mr. Washington had spoken in that city before. Among other illustrations of this progress, he mentioned the fact that no less than 100 telephones are used by the colored people of that city in their homes and places of business. In conclusion he said: "Our colored citizens are too busy to meddle with politics, though they have two representatives in the city legislature."

Although colored people vote in Tennessee, they do not seem to be represented in the city or state governments outside of Chattanooga. Nashville, however, has a company of Negro firemen who have been in service in that city for more than 30 years. Knoxville has four colored policemen, and in Clarksville it is said that all the letter carriers in the city are colored.

Among professional men, Negro doctors, dentists and pharmacists seem to have been unusually successful in Tennessee. There are about 200 Negro physicians in Tennessee, of whom about 165 or 170 have graduated from the Meharry medical school at Nashville. Nashville has 30 colored physicians, four colored dentists and four colored drug stores. Memphis has something over 30 physicians, and maintains a flourishing local colored medical society, which is doing considerable service in the effort to improve the sanitary conditions of those parts of the city in which the majority of the Negro population live. Everywhere throughout the state the visit of Mr. Washington and his party created the most profound interest, both among colored and white people. Nowhere was it possible to obtain an auditorium large enough to hold the immense crowds that thronged to hear him speak, not even in the Ryman auditorium in Nashville which holds 8,000 people.[13]

Perhaps witnessing the acquisition of skills and property by African Americans made Park feel confident that they were "separate" but progressing within their own caste.

Although many sociologists posited racist explanations for the socio-economic status of most African Americans as late as 1930, Boas's recontextualization of the empirical data of nineteenth-century anthropology generated internal conceptual stresses on the issue of African Americans' racial capabilities and fostered an interest in the social-structural changes that were perceptibly transforming the demographic character of the northern urban and industrial areas in which most sociologists lived and worked. In other words, there was no monocausal relation between the rise of naturalism in post-1910 sociology and the decline of racist views in that discipline. Prior internal conceptual stresses—exacerbated by Boasian anthropology in the years before 1911—and contemporaneous social changes were *necessary*, not to say sufficient, conditions for the development of progressive theories of race and race relations. Furthermore, during the years 1910 to 1919 there were forces pushing and pulling blacks out of the South into the urban-industrial areas in the North where most competent sociologists taught. The push came from oppressive and exploitive conditions in the South—not only the widespread legal and extralegal violence perpetrated against blacks but also extreme economic discrimination. The chief pull was the North's shortage of unskilled labor. The northward migration of blacks had increased steadily from 1870 through 1910; by 1915, when World War I began to impede the flow of cheap labor from Europe and many immigrants returned to their homelands to take part in the conflict, larger numbers of blacks were recruited to take their place in northern industries. Even more arrived after 1917 when industries expanded as the United States entered the conflict. The net increase in the northern black population from 1910 to 1920 is estimated at 800,000 to 1,000,000 persons. The effect after 1920 was to nationalize the so-called Negro problem, to precipitate black racial consciousness as manifested in Marcus Garvey's "back to Africa" movement, and to stimulate the development of progressive sociological theories by African Americans on race and race relations.

As early as 1913, the *Annals of the American Academy of Political and Social Science* published an issue devoted to the study of blacks, titled "The Negro's Progress in Fifty Years." Contributors included black sociologists George E. Haynes, R.R. Wright Jr., W.E.B. Du Bois, Monroe N. Work, and Kelly Miller, and northern white sociologists James P. Lichtenberger and Robert E. Park. Their articles drew on empirical evidence to buttress their argument that blacks had made tremendous progress since emancipation. Their empirical world view, in essence, reinforced their progressive evolutionist theory.

Black sociologists were especially fascinated by the progress brought about by the urbanization of blacks in both the North and the South. George E. Haynes—who had received his doctorate from Columbia University in 1912, had worked for the National Urban League, and would later teach economics and sociology at Fisk University—saw tremendous obstacles confronting blacks in the cities but argued that the "successes . . . in both industry and trade are multiplying and with substantial encouragement may change the rule to exception in the teeth of excessive handicaps." He went on to assert that "judging from the studies of Negro enterprises made in Philadelphia and in New York City and from widespread attendance upon the annual meetings of the National Negro Business League, substantial progress is triumphing over unusual obstacles."[14]

That most of the blacks migrating to northern cities were unskilled laborers did not daunt the proponents of progress. R. R. Wright Jr., an African Methodist Episcopal minister who had received his doctorate in sociology from the University of Pennsylvania in 1912, expressed optimism concerning the prospects for black unskilled labor in northern cities. Whereas the skilled laborer, he said, had difficulty finding work,

> the Negro unskilled laborer has been a welcome guest. In nearly every large city, special employment agencies have been opened in order to induce Negro workers from the South to come North, where there is abundant public work to be done, on the streets, sewers, filter plants, subways, railroads, etc. Negro hodcarriers have almost driven whites out of business in some cities, while as teamsters, firemen and street cleaners, they are more and more in demand. In the hotel business, the Negro is in demand in the large cities, as waiter, bellman, etc., while the Negro women are more and more in demand as domestic servants.[15]

To Wright, the suggestion that the mass of black unskilled labor was stagnant was fallacious because of the "degree of respect given much unskilled work among Negroes." Instead, he argued, "this group of unskilled workers has shared something of the progress of the group."[16]

The idea that black progress was not restricted to unskilled labor and business was documented in W.E.B. Du Bois's article "The Negro in Literature and Art." Weighing the achievements and progress of blacks against discrimination in those vocations, Du Bois concluded: "So the sum of accomplishment is but an imperfect indication of what the Negro race is capable of in America and in the world."[17]

Robert E. Park's article tried to account for the improvement in the home life and the standard of living among blacks. He drew distinctions between the different classes of blacks and insisted that in order to understand "the social standards, the degree of culture and comfort which the Negro peasant, the Negro artisan, and business and professional man enjoy today," one had "to take account of those earlier ante-bellum conditions out of which they sprang." For the vast majority of blacks, whose progenitors were fieldhands, conditions varied according to the locale in which they lived. Park described the homes of black peasants in southwestern Virginia and the Sea Islands of South Carolina as "comfortable" but depicted those in the up-country of Alabama as "rude huts." Nonetheless, there were black farmers in both the North and the South who had achieved a high standard of living. One farmer in Edwardsville, Kansas, had erected a modern house that Park described as a "twenty-two room palace overlooking a 503 acre farm." Typical of the black artisans who were descendants of antebellum skilled workers was a man who lived in what Park called "a neat five-room cottage," which he owned. The black middle class, descended from free blacks and privileged slaves in Charleston, Baltimore, Washington, Philadelphia, New York City, and New Orleans, lived in "comfortable" homes. Although Park admitted that in all large cities and in all small southern towns there were blacks who lived "meanly and miserably," he still believed there was cause for optimism. "The Negro," Park concluded, "has made great progress in many directions during the past half century, but nowhere more so than in his home, and nowhere, it may be added, do the fruits of education show to better advantage than in the home of the educated Negro."[18]

If many African Americans were progressing, even in the South, and demonstrating that they were equal to whites, why did the caste line persist? Park attempted to answer this question during the Tuskegee years by analyzing prejudice. The "chief obstacle" to the assimilation of blacks and Asians, he said, was "not mental traits but physical traits." African Americans and Asians were prevented from sharing in the social life of most white Americans because they were "distinguished by certain external marks" that furnished a "permanent physical substratum upon which and around which the irritations and animosities, incidental to all human intercourse, tend to accumulate and so gain strength and volume."[19]

If this sort of race prejudice was the main obstacle to breaking down the caste line, how could it be done away with? When Park readied himself to leave Tuskegee and enter upon his teaching career, he seemed to think that no amount of human intervention could alter the antagonism that had developed between whites and blacks. In a short unpublished paper, "Southern Sentiment and Southern Policy toward the Negro," he considered the possibility of altering the relations between the races through northern "intervention and legalistic means." The year 1913, Park surmised,

> will probably be remembered by the colored people of the United States as one of mixed blessings. As I have travelled about the country I have had an opportunity [to] talk with colored people in all walks of life in all parts of the country and I have found the conviction very general that, some have, quietly, and without anything in particular to indicate it, that a decided change has taken place or is taking place, in the situation of the Negro in this century.
>
> For one thing my attention [was] more than once called to the fact, in the year 1913, at the time that we are celebrating the fiftieth anniversary of our freedom, the Negroes are exercising less influence and are having less part in government of the country than any time since the Civil War.
>
> Another thing to which my attention has been called is the fact while in 1913 there was probably less crime, fewer lynchings and even homes built among Negroes in proportion to the population than ever before, it was the year in which all that remained of the Civil Rights Bill [of 1875], the law which attempted to secure for Negroes equal privileges with white men in hotels, theaters, and public conveyances was finally erased from the Federal statute books.
>
> Most of the people with whom I have talked have a theory about this matter. They say this indicates that the Negro is losing ground in this century, that in [the] North, especially, there is less interest in the welfare and progress of the Negro than there was; and that, as a result of this indifference the Negro has been abandoned to those people in the South who are anxious to reduce him to a condition little better than slavery.
>
> It seems to me that the situation is not so simple as it has been described. In the first place there are some things that laws can not give and on the other hand there are some things that the law can not take away. And this applies just as much to laws that are passed to support and protect the Negro as it does to laws that are passed to oppress him and hold him down.
>
> One thing which law can not control is sentiment. If there is prejudice against the Negro, law can not remove it. On the other hand an unjust law, no matter against whom it is directed, will in the long run work injury to the whole community and the sentiment of the community will not support it.[20]

For Park, in other words, it was impossible to legislate racial morality, for the law was almost powerless when it ran counter to sentiments.

His skepticism was phrased another way in some notes he composed after arriving at the University of Chicago. On September 12, 1913, Park wrote in reference to the sentiments of whites that "in spite of all the progress of [the] Negro and the efforts of philanthropy to lift the general level of intelligence and culture . . . it has not given promise of success in the struggle to make the Negro practically efficient and morally equal with the white man."[21] According to Park, the white man's skepticism stemmed from his estimate of the blacks' capabilities and his sheer superordinate relationship to blacks in reference to power. "The white man's arrogance," he concluded, was "a product of his dealing with people whom he feels are inferior and over which he tends to exercise despotic control."[22]

Nevertheless, in Park's theory blacks were significant actors. Although the caste-like system in the South was "fostered by the policy of the dominant race," Park believed that it had actually begun as "a spontaneous movement on the part of both" races. The caste line affected the black population significantly by ensuring the development of a "common interest among all the different colors and classes of the race." Park believed that the sentiment of solidarity among blacks, which facilitated the development of a nationality, was a "response and accommodation to changing internal and external conditions." The emergence of separate churches, schools, libraries, hospitals, and towns affecting social conditions in the South, Park thought, was evidence that the "races seem to be tending in the direction of a biracial organization of society, in which the Negro is gradually gaining a limited autonomy."[23] Although Park was hesitant to predict the "ultimate outcome of this movement," he believed that certain benefits accrued to the African American leadership class as a result of caste barriers. "In a biracial organization," he declared, those leaders "obtain much greater prominence, according as they are able to control their own people. . . . This makes Dr. Rev. Hall a power in Chicago. Segregation plays into his hand. His power grows out of the fact that, being a Negro he only has to be superior to Negroes [in order] to stand high with the white. This, always provided he represents the whites."[24]

In short, unlike the southern sociologists of this period, Park did not embrace the view that the mental abilities of blacks vis-à-vis whites adversely affected race relations. For him, the nature of those relations was determined by the types of contact between the two races. Nevertheless, Park was no revolutionary (in fact, he was a conservative); rather, like Boas, he was a transitional figure, caught between the biological determinism of the social Darwinists and the new cultural determinism. Consequently, during the years between 1913 and 1928, biological determinism intruded perceptibly into Park's theory of biracial organization in his famous (or perhaps infamous) theory of racial temperaments and his continuing analysis of prejudice.

Like the southern sociologists, Park thought racial prejudice was instinctive. Contradicting his 1913 assertion that it was a reaction to physical traits, however, he now held that racial prejudice was a response to the scarcity of resources. Park wrote in 1917 that the main stimulus was competition: "Race prejudice may be regarded as a spontaneous more or less instinctive defense reaction, the practical effect of which is to restrict free competition. Its importance as a social function is due to the fact that free competition, particularly between people with different standards of living, seems to be, if not the original source, at least the stimulus to which prejudice is the response." Since racial competition would be restricted in a biracial organization of society, racial prejudice would disappear, and there would be "no obstacle to racial cooperation."[25]

Park, in other words, concurred in the argument of the progressives that no racial impediments prevented the black population from producing a middle class whose size was proportionately equal to the size of the white middle class. But Park also believed the southern argument that blacks and whites could not compete in the same marketplace—primarily because he believed in the concepts of an "instinctive" prejudice, "the mores," and "the racial temperament." Thus, in 1928 Park represented race relations since emancipation as having changed from a situation in which all whites held a socio-economic status superior to that of all blacks:

ALL WHITE
ALL COLORED

to one in which there was both social and occupational differentiation, despite the persistence of a caste line that "maintained" social distances:

White	*Colored*
Professional Occupation	Professional Occupation
Business Occupation	Business Occupation
Labor	Labor

"The races," Park concluded, "no longer look up and down: they look across."[26]

As late as 1931, Park was convinced that a so-called "separate but equal" society, built on the Washingtonian model of industrial education, had reached fruition and thereby benefited African Americans. On May 20, 1931, in a University of Chicago course titled "The Negro in America," he told his class that:

> Washington's product has wrought a true change in the South. [The] Southern white has a respect for him. Washington really represented the freeman. [Blacks are] beginning to own property, to settle down, and enter into occupations. [He] built churches; got expression for his own life. [There] was no middle class . . . only (1) educated negroes

and (2) freedmen. Washington inspired this group which was enter-
ing business. [Washington] established "Farmer's Conference." . . .
[He] invited negro farmers, teachers, . . . had farmers telling what was
condition of churches, schools, farms, and relations with whites in
their sections. What improvement is going on? Who is buying land?
[Washington] always gave preference to ones who had bought land.[27]

Between 1937 and 1939, however, Park reformulated his theory. Impressed
by social structural changes that affected the black population and by his experiences abroad, he declared in 1939:

> The same forces which brought about the diversity of races will in-
> evitably bring about in the long run, a diversity in the peoples in the
> modern world corresponding to that which we have seen in the old. It
> is likely, however, that these diversities will be based in the future less
> on inheritance and race and rather more on culture and occupation.
> That means that race conflicts in the modern world, which is already
> or presently will be a single great society, will be more in the future
> confused with, and eventually superseded by, the conflicts of classes.[28]

Park's emphasis on the interaction between the class and race variables and
his prediction concerning the eventual saliency of class in American race relations foreshadowed William J. Wilson's position. Park envisioned a near
future marked by racial conflict and struggle—as more African Americans
elevated their status, they would meet resistance from whites—but was confident that this phase, though inevitable, would pass. Thus he wrote in
1943: "The races and people which fate has brought together in America
and within the limits of the larger world economy will continue, in the
emerging world society, their struggle for a political and a racial equality
that was denied them in the world that is passing."[29]

The view of W. Lloyd Warner and his associates, however, differed
from that of Park. Formulated primarily on conditions in the Deep South,
Warner in 1936 represented race relations as in the accompanying diagram.

He predicted that the caste line might possibly assume a vertical position (D–E), but if so, "the class situation in either group would not be
fundamentally disturbed, except that the top Negro group would be equivalent with the top white, while the lower classes in each of the parallel
groups would also be equivalent."[30] In short, Warner thought the biracial
organization Park had diagrammed in 1928 might yet come into existence.
For him, class was an important aspect of race relations and would remain
so in the foreseeable future. Yet despite the possibility of economic parity,
race would always be the salient variable in American race relations.

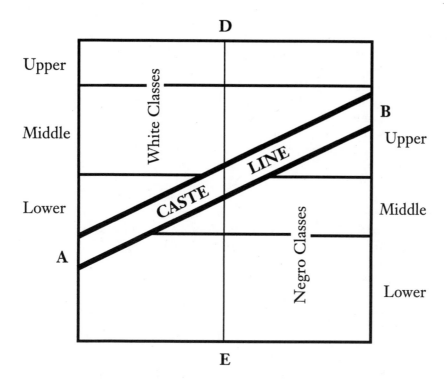

Believing that there were structural impediments to the fruition of an assimilated society, Warner preached a pessimistic philosophy suggesting that caste would remain a salient variable in American race relations. Although his arguments were buried underneath the assimilationist onslaught until the 1960s, his dismal prophecies concerning the persistence of caste-like barriers in the American social order seem plausible in these days of racial conflict. It should be remembered, however, as Alphonso Pinkney clearly recognizes, that a belief in the permanence of caste in American life serves to some extent to rationalize a laissez-faire, do-nothing approach to circumstances that are in fact subject to the intervention of the human will.

The triumph of Park's position on the assimilation of African Americans and its persistence until about 1970 were due, for the most part, to the ability of distinguished African American sociologists such as E. Franklin Frazier, Charles S. Johnson, and William Oscar Brown (although they drew a distinction between ethnic relations and race relations and believed that assimilation would not occur in the immediate future) and white scholars such as Louis Wirth to sustain the plausibility of Park's ethnic cycle. Challenges to the dominant point of view, however, emanated from left-liberal students of Boas, such as the anthropologist Melville J. Herskovits and the University of Chicago–trained Marxist of African American ancestry, Oliver C. Cox.

During the mid-1930s and 1940s, in response to Park's assertion that African culture had been destroyed in the New World, Herskovits (drawing on a turn-of-the-century hypothesis of W.E.B. Du Bois) had argued that African culture did survive in varying degrees among African Americans in such forms as etiquette, music, religion, cuisine, and speech.[31] Although this thesis was attacked by most competent social scientists of the period—particularly E. Franklin Frazier and Gunnar Myrdal—it had an emotional impact: it suggested to African Americans that traditions and values passed on from their despised ancestors were in fact significant ways of life that deserved protection—and the price of losing this valuable heritage, which would be destroyed through complete assimilation, would be too high.

Herskovits's emphasis on Africanism in the African American population was a minority position in the social sciences for approximately thirty years. His thesis was revised and modified, however, during the heyday of the "Black Power" revolt in the late 1960s and has persisted in an adulterated form as an integral part of the argument of many social scientists (both African American and Euro-American) who insist that most African Americans have a distinctive world view. For these persons, culture, not class, is the salient variable in American race relations and, therefore, the key to any social engineering schemes concocted by the ruling class. Herskovits, in essence, provided the cultural foundation for nation-based theory.

Unlike left-liberals such as Herskovits and Ruth Benedict, conservatives such as Park and Warner, and socialists such as Gunnar Myrdal, the African American Marxist Oliver Cromwell Cox was critical of approaches to race relations which did not see racial prejudice, caste, and racism (terms often used interchangeably before 1945) as products of the institutional functioning of a capitalist society. "Race prejudice," Cox argued cogently in 1948, "constitutes an attitudinal justification necessary for an easy exploitation of some race. . . . Race prejudice is the social-attitudinal concomitant of the racial-exploitative practice in a capitalistic society. The substance of race prejudice is the exploitation of the militarily weaker race."[32]

Since Cox wrote his *Caste, Class, and Race: A Study of Social Dynamics,* some African Americans have made considerable gains, as Wilson noted in 1978, by moving themselves into the middle class; a few have even entered the ruling class. Nevertheless, the question remains: will an African American ethnic identity, regardless of class and status, determine whether many of the present generation (between the ages of fifteen and thirty-five) will have equal access to wealth, privilege, loyalty, respect, and power in the near future? Or will they be deemed scapegoats in the United States of America's perilous future?

Conclusion

Since the 1970s, Boasian thought has given rise to numerous and diverse themes on race and race relations. For those scholars who constitute most of the antiracist branch of American intellectuals, Boasian thought suggests that the concept of race is a "folk classification," which—to use Audrey Smedley's words—"continues in large part because of its value as a mechanism for indentifying who should have access to wealth, privilege, loyalty, respect, and power and who should not. . . . It is a powerful psychological force, providing scapegoat functions as well as a facile external means of establishing and measuring one's own self-worth."[1] Scholars such as Smedley, believe that persons should be judged and treated according to their merits as individuals. Yet racist scholars too can draw sustenance from Boas. Since he believed that the average level of achievement in blacks, because of their inferior cranial capacities, was lower than the average in whites, and because he offered a "men of high genius" hypothesis, his work can be drawn on to support the elitist racial determism most recently appearing in the works of Arthur R. Jensen, Pat Shipman, and Charles Murray and the late Richard Herrnstein. For them, racial intellectual differences are real.

In the field of race relations within the discipline of sociology, the implications of Boasian thought have also been two-pronged. On the one hand, Boas's prescriptive statement suggesting the desirability of the assimilation of blacks and whites has given us two conflicting stratification theories; these present two different answers to the question of whether race or class is the more salient variable in American race relations, as borne out in the dispute between William J. Wilson and Alphonso Pinkney in the 1980s. On the other hand, Boasian thought on Africa has influenced cultural pluralists. Its pessimistic manifestation can be found in the work of Afrocentrists such as Molefi K. Asante, while its optimistic variety suffuses the work of Henry Louis Gates, Jr.

In sum, Boas's ideas have survived his times. In our confusing days his ideas have import for race, and race relations; they are as significant in our day as they were in his.

Appendix
Toward an Ecumenical Mythistory

In a presidential address to the American Historical Association in 1985, the distinguished world historian William H. McNeill announced that since the 1960s "the scope and range of historiography has widened, and that change looks as irreversible . . . as the widening of physics that occurred when Einstein's equations proved capable of explaining phenomena that Newton's could not." McNeill doubted that African Americans, women, Asians, Africans, and Amerindians would be excluded "from any future mythistory of the world" and thought it "impossible not to believe" that the new mythistories represented "an advance on older notions." Nevertheless, he suggested, only "time would settle" the issue of whether or not he was correct.[1]

In light of the recent historiography dealing with the treatment of African Americans in the American social sciences, McNeill was indeed correct. The history of the social science of race relations, a subfield of American intellectual history, is perhaps telling Americans more about themselves on the issue of race—most of which they are reluctant to hear—than any other subfield in recent American history. The fundamental question confronting these historians and historically minded social scientists is whether or not the pre-1945 social scientific scholarship can provide insight and guidance on present-day issues of race in general and of racial and ethnic groups in particular. In answering this complex question, they have focused primarily on the work of Franz Boas (a German-Jewish immigrant) and his students in anthropology at Columbia University; the Chicago school of race relations dominated by the theories of Robert Ezra Park (an American of British descent); and the liberal orthodoxy of moral immediatism, liberal globalism, and social engineering that permeated the work of Gunnar Myrdal (a Swede). Through their theories and the influence of their associates and former graduate students, their thought dominated the social science disciplines from the 1930s until the 1970s.

It is no miracle, then, that the work of these three figures on race in general and African Americans in particular has initiated a hot debate concerning their significance and influence. Although Charles Silberman

103

wrote in 1965 that "Negro-white relations have entered a new and radically different stage—a stage so different from the past as to make familiar approaches and solutions obsolete, irrelevant, and sometimes even harmful,"[2] I think there is some fundamental, lasting soundness in the thought of the three pioneers of the social science of race relations. In fact, I would argue that only by understanding the pre-1945 social scientific scholarship on African Americans can we come to an understanding of their potential condition(s) and destiny in the twenty-first century—in which numerous diverse groups will vociferously demand greater status and power.

For more than five decades, historically minded anthropologists and intellectual historians have celebrated the decisive role that Franz Uri Boas played in undermining the racist world view that prevailed in the social sciences during the years before 1930.[3] Surprisingly little of this literature—especially when one considers the quantity of readily accessible data—deals with Boas's specific treatment of African Americans. Most of these scholars were content to assume (erroneously) that Boas treated African Americans much like the "primitives" he studied: that is, with a great deal of affection. The small body of literature that comment on Boas's attitudes toward African Americans has largely ignored what I term "the Boasian paradox": that is, the contradiction between the inferences based on his physical anthropology and his liberal values. This contradiction, I have argued, is not surprising when one considers his life and career, ethnicity, the historical context, and the controversies surrounding issues concerning the condition and destiny of Africans.[4] For indeed, like most scholars—albeit to lesser extent—Boas was a prisoner of his times.

In an article published in *Isis* in 1973, the historian Edward H. Beardsley examined and analyzed the historical treatment of Boas by students and colleagues during the previous thirty years. Unlike those anthropologists, who believed that Boas's revulsion against antiblack racism was fundamentally motivated by his liberal values and directly related to his ethnic status as a German-born Jew in America, Beardsley argued that the "most basic and fundamental explanation" was "his commitment to scientific objectivity and reliability." Although Boas was "from a Jewish background and a foe of anti-Semitism since his youth," Beardsley nevertheless pointed out that "Boas did not become actively and publicly involved on that issue until the 1920s, when Nazi racists made a major effort to enlist science in support of their views." Furthermore, Boas "never involved himself with the Indian's plight as he did with the Negro's or Jew's," primarily because "the idea of Indian inferiority was never a major tenet of scientific racism."[5] As a consequence, Beardsley vociferously argued that "Boas was an activist for what were essentially professional reasons."[6]

Four years later Hasia R. Diner challenged both the Boasian anthro-
pologists and Beardsley, when she argued in her book *In the Almost
Promised Land: Jews and Blacks, 1915–1935* that there was truth in both of
their contentions. Boas wrote for "social as well as for scientific reasons,"
Diner stated. "He was deeply concerned with the real human suffering
created by racist thinking and eagerly shared his findings with the
NAACP." It is Diner's thesis that the fundamental reason Boas wrote about
African Americans was his ethnic status as a liberal, German-born Jew in
America who believed that blacks and Jews had a common bond of suffering. He was not naive about his own group's self-interest in discrediting
antiblack racism: "The same principles which Boas and his students used to
discredit antiblack thinking," Diner concluded, "could be employed as effective weapons to combat anti-Jewish sentiment."[7]

The idea that Boas's skeptical stance toward antiblack racism stemmed
from his desire to protect his own group was extended by Marshall Hyatt in
his timely biography, *Franz Boas—Social Activist: The Dynamics of Ethnicity*,
published in 1990. In his 1894 address as vice-president of Section H of the
American Association for the Advancement of Science in Brooklyn, New
York, "Boas used blacks as a surrogate to avoid charges of scientific bias," in
his biographer's opinion:

> The timing of the polemic against prejudice is instructive. Having
> recently tangled with Washington, [D.C.,] the center of white Anglo-
> Saxon Protestant-controlled anthropological study, over the museum
> appointment, Boas was still licking his wounds. . . . Boas conceivably
> read the incident in ethnic terms. Given his heightened sensitivity to
> persecution, which colored much of his life in Germany, and the domi-
> nant influence of white, Anglo-Saxon Protestants in anthropology, this
> is not surprising. Accordingly, he began his assault on prejudice soon
> after his disappointment over the Columbian Museum job. However,
> rather than call attention to his own plight and risk accusations of sub-
> jectivity, Boas chose another aspect, that directed against Afro-
> Americans, at which to vent his distress. This camouflage became part
> of Boas's raison d'etre for attacking all forms of human prejudice.[8]

Nevertheless, "it was in the area of race," Hyatt concludes, "that Boas had
his greatest impact on America and on future intellectual thought."[9] Yet,
ironically, nowhere does Hyatt explore the relationship between Boas and
Booker T. Washington, W.E.B. Du Bois, R.R. Wright Sr., George
Washington Ellis, Carter G. Woodson, Alain LeRoy Locke, Charles S.
Johnson, George E. Haynes, Abram Harris, Monroe N. Work, and
Charles H. Thompson. Investigation into Boas's correspondence with
these major African American intellectuals would have qualified Hyatt's

argument that Boas's indictment of the plight of Afro-Americans was mere camouflage for attacking anti-Semitism.

Carl N. Degler's *In Search of Human Nature: The Decline and Revival of Darwinism in American Social Thought* (1991) concurs in Hyatt's argument that Boas was a progressive on the issue of the equipotentiality of African Americans. Arguing "that Boas did not arrive at" his position on African Americans "from a disinterested, scientific inquiry" but that his ideas "derived from an ideological commitment that began in his early life and academic experiences in Europe and continued in America," Degler discounts Boas's equivocal and racist statements.[10] "Nowhere," he says, "does Boas' commitment to the ideology of equal opportunity and the recognition of the worth of oppressed or ignored people become more evident than in his relation to Afro-Americans, a people whose life patterns had long been allegedly 'accounted for' by race." Degler uses as evidence for his position Boas's attempt to raise money from Andrew Carnegie "to support a new Museum on the Negro and the African Past"; Boas's 1906 address on the African past at the commencement of Atlanta University, which had such a profound impact on the thought of W.E.B. Du Bois; and his discussion of the ramifications of white-black intermarriage.[11] Although such arguments seem compelling, it should be noted that Degler, unlike Hyatt, ignores the racist physical anthropology that was in tension with Boas's liberal ideology, and neither Hyatt nor Degler shows how that tension was exacerbated by the increasing migration of blacks from the southeastern states to New York, bringing what was thought to be a peculiar southern problem to the doorsteps of anthropologists in the urban-industrial North. In short, until the influence of social-structural changes on Boas is investigated there can be little understanding of the complex paradoxes in this transitional figure's thought.

Elazar Barkan, in *The Retreat of Scientific Racism: Changing Concepts of Race in Britain and the United States between the World Wars* (1992), denied the existence of these paradoxes. Asserting that Boas was a racial egalitarian whose "political beliefs" were more salient than his "scientific commitments," Barkan constructed a nonsensical argument: "Boas was no racist, but he did reflect the values of his society."[12] Further investigation into Boas's writings on African Americans would have revealed the tension between his lifelong belief in inherent racial differences and his commitment to cultural explanations of human behavior, between his political beliefs and scientific commitments, and between the science of physical anthropology and his liberal values. Put another way, although Boas certainly believed that African Americans had a defective ancestry as a result of having smaller cranial cavities than those of Euro-Americans, he did not think that should be used as an excuse to exclude them as individuals from participating as much as their capacity allowed in the community or nation-state.

Since the 1960s, scholars of race and race relations have been engaged in two major debates in reference to Robert E. Park's theories: first, whether Park was a proponent of racial determinism; second, whether he was an advocate of assimilation. Since Park was not a systematic thinker, these debates have been marred by the subjective valuations made by the various adversaries.

Although scholars agree that Park was one of the first social scientists to subordinate racial-determinist explanations of human behavior to social or cultural ones, it should be noted that in 1918 Park penned a concept of "racial temperaments" as follows: "Everywhere and always the Negro has been interested rather in expression than in action; interested in life itself than in its reconstruction or reformation. The Negro is, by natural disposition, neither an intellectual nor idealist like the Jew, nor a brooding introspective like the East Indian, nor a pioneer and frontiersman like the Anglo-Saxon. He is primarily an artist, loving life for its own sake. His metier is expression rather than action. The Negro is, so to speak, the lady among the races."[13]

The late Ralph Ellison and the sociologist John H. Stanfield II have branded this concept as racist. Stanfield, for example, argued persuasively in 1985 that "biological determinism was apparent in his [Park's] concept of 'racial temperaments,' which he believed was the factor behind the so-called cultural uniqueness among blacks."[14] On the other hand, scholars such as Morris Janowitz, César Graña, and, most recently, Barbara Ballis Lal have sought to excuse or justify Park's attention to "racial temperament." In *The Romance of Culture in an Urban Civilization: Robert E. Park on Race and Ethnic Relations in the Cities* (1990), Barbara Ballis Lal declared: "Park rejected Social Darwinism, all its implications regarding the biological basis of cultural differences and its belief that racial stratification reflected a 'natural order' of selection and fitness." Furthermore, Park's "emphasis upon race relations, rather than the alleged hereditary attributes of races, . . . suggests that the influence he accorded to racial temperaments was very limited."[15]

In 1992 Stanford M. Lyman, who has treated the concept in "relation to his [Park's] larger discussion of assimilation and the problems attending the modern civilizational process," attempted to resolve the debate: "What Park seems to have been doing in his invocation of a racial temperament is attempting to respecify, in as exact a way as his knowledge and observation would allow, precisely what amount of the Negro's character and personality was biological in origin, what amount a survival of African culture, and what amount a product of acculturation in America. Furthermore, Park sought to get at the effects that the internalization of this tripartite and emergent compound of constitutional elements, cultural survivals, acculturative adaptations would have on the incorporation of African Americans into an ever modernizing United States of America." Nevertheless, Lyman admits that "in the end, the precise weight that should be assigned respectively to hereditary and acculturative factors eluded Park."[16]

My reading of Park suggests that at that juncture in his career he saw a fundamental hereditary basis for the African Americans' racial temperament, and their temperament as an obstacle to their assimilation. Like Franz Boas, Park was a transitional figure, caught between racial determinism and the trend toward cultural and social determinism; his thought on the character and capabilities of African Americans and the nature of prejudice was uneven. Peter Kivisto, in reference to deficiencies in Lal's work, summed up the matter quite aptly in 1992: "Indicative of the fact that the [Park's] break [with biological determinism] was not entirely ambiguous was his occasional relapse to the language of instincts as well as his unfortunate characterization of African Americans as 'the lady among races.'"[17]

The second debate surrounding Park's theories centers on whether he was an advocate of assimilation. Historians and historically minded social scientists of American race relations have virtually ignored Park's concept of a biracial organization of society, despite the fact that the concept was central to his explanation of black-white relations for more than twenty-five years. Perhaps most post-Myrdalian scholars of race relations concurred in E. Franklin Frazier's 1947 criticism: the theory of a biracial organization of society, he argued persuasively, was a "static theory of race relations. His [Park's] theory not only contained the fatalism inherent in Sumner's concept of mores. His theory was originally based upon the assumption that the races could not mix and mingle freely."[18]

Ironically, in 1981 R. Fred Wacker published a small volume arguing that Park's biracial theory was his *true* theory of white-black relations. Seeking to educate the revisionists of the 1960s who believed that social scientists such as Park thought "all groups would shed their distinctive cultures and become WASPs," Wacker declared: "My study of the ideas and attitudes of Robert Park leads me to conclude that he did not believe all minority groups in America would be assimilated." In reference to Park's theory of a "biracial organization," he stated that Park "did not predict the outcome of conflict and competition." Believing that Park was a pluralist, Wacker argued that Park, like Horace Kallen, a cultural pluralist, was focusing on "groups and group needs" and thereby rejecting "the individualistic perspective of most social scientists." Furthermore, Wacker stated unequivocally that Park saw "the rise and revitalization of ethnic and racial consciousness as a natural response to prejudice and domination." In other words, for Park, "racial consciousness was part of a movement toward mental health."[19]

Unlike Wacker, the historically minded sociologist John H. Stanfield II has made a compelling case for the validity of labeling Park an assimilationist. Taking to task Wacker's view of Park as an advocate of the intrinsic worth of black consciousness, Stanfield stated in *Philanthropy and Jim Crow in American Social Science* (1985): "Since Park presumed the assimilation of physically dissimilar groups was problematic yet inevitable, it followed that segregated black communities were necessarily temporary, and, therefore, that race consciousness was also temporary." Stanfield was critical of Park's view of race consciousness as a temporary response to oppression—insofar as Park "did not consider the normality of race consciousness in dominant as well as in subordinate populations. Since Park did not consider race consciousness as a form of enculturation in a racially stratified society," Stanfield concludes that he not only "ushered into sociological literature an a-cultural and an a-sociological conception of race consciousness" but "set the stage for succeeding generations of sociologists to view black race consciousness negatively as a product of antagonistic relations with whites, which materialized through conscious white racism and the formation of ghettos."[20]

Stanfield's criticisms of Park, as he clearly recognizes, are ahistorical and thus leave unanswered the question of whether Park deserves a place among the key figures in the discussion of the condition and destiny of African Americans. A work that avoids Stanfield's debunking is the revised edition of John Higham's *Send These to Me*. In his monumental essay "Ethnic Pluralism in American Thought" the distinguished social and intellectual historian has restored Park to his rightful historical place in the history of race relations experts. Reconciling the debate between the positions represented by Wacker and Stanfield, Higham demonstrated that Robert Ezra Park made two modifications in the "classic American ideal of assimilation": first, he extended the ideal "to include Negroes, as well as immigrants; second, he gave it [the concept of assimilation] an international and fully interracial formulation; he also incorporated within it a quasi-pluralistic appreciation." In short, "Park interpreted the problems of a multiethnic society," Higham correctly concludes, "in a way that took account of pluralist as well as assimilationist claims." Park's broad international vision, Higham points out, was not applied by his successors.

Ignoring Herskovits's Boasian emphasis on African retentions in the African American population, and relying instead on Frazier's judgments, Higham argues that Gunnar Myrdal's *An American Dilemma* represented the renationalization of Park's international "melting pot."[21]

In 1987 Stow Persons qualified the arguments of Stanfield and Higham and suggested that Park struggled with "the problem of assimilation as well as his growing doubts about its inevitability." Toward the end of Park's life, Persons noted, Park believed that "the potentialities of a rational and humane order could be realized only if people become thoroughly familiar with one another's characteristics and problems. . . . Park knew that any such achievement was remote."[22] More recently, sociologists such as James B. McKee and Stanford M. Lyman have also noted Park's doubts about the inevitability of assimilation in the near future. In one of his last papers, McKee has stressed, "Park gave to his fellow sociologists an image of a racial future marked by militant action, conflict, and possible violence, instead of one of gradual, peaceful change leading to increased tolerance and social acceptance."[23] For Lyman, Park's later works indicated that the struggle between races was "inevitable even if its outcome was less certain."[24]

Most scholars involved in the discourse on Robert Ezra Park, in short, treat his thought as if it were static, whereas my research indicates that Park's theories evolved during his long lifetime. Between 1905 and 1913 he contributed to Booker T. Washington's myths in reference to race and race relations, while also recontextualizing and universalizing scientific racist data concerning the socioeconomic status of blacks. During his tenure at the University of Chicago from 1913 to 1932, Park occasionally lapsed into reversals and transvaluations but, perceiving the influences of Franz Boas and the Great Migration, continued to recontextualize his analyses of race, prejudice, and race relations. Finally, during the years 1932 to 1943, under the impact of the evidence of black progress and his travels abroad, Park adopted an "alternative ideology," one defined by Nancy Leys Stepan and Sander L. Gilman as a "radically different world view, with different perceptions of reality goals and points of reference."[25] Understanding Park's transition from a view of African Americans as a homogeneous race to a perspective in which racial status and class are increasingly confused will enable us, in short, to understand why current debates on these issues assume such volatility.

What Higham calls "the ideational approach to social issues" began to dominate the social sciences with the publication of Myrdal's work in 1944. The how and whys of this occurrence are the subject of Walter A. Jackson's *Gunnar Myrdal and America's Conscience: Social Engineering and Racial*

Liberalism, 1931–1987 (1991): "*An American Dilemma* . . . emerged from a complex process of interaction between this politically minded intellectual and a foundation, a community of American social scientists, broader currents of political, social, and economic change." Jackson traces Myrdal's life from his youth in Dalarna, Sweden, to his death in 1987, arguing that Myrdal's commitment to social engineering and moral reform grew out of the egalitarianism and moral values of his childhood and his fascination with the rationalism of the Enlightenment. Jackson notes, however, that "there remained in his thought a tension between his commitment to equality and his infatuation with an elitist conception of social engineering." In short, when Myrdal arrived in the United States in 1938, he "brought a conception of social science as a process of moral inquiry and a belief that social engineering" was the primary goal of the social sciences.[26]

The Carnegie Corporation, which chose Myrdal to conduct the race relations research for *An American Dilemma*, took the initiative away from the American social scientists who were writing for small audiences and placed it in the hands of a "pragmatic problem solver who promised to come up with a fresh approach in a book aimed at a broad audience of educated Americans."[27] By co-opting centrist, liberal, and radical social scientists, Myrdal created a consensus behind a liberal analysis of race relations in America.

During his travels in the South and in northern urban ghettos, Myrdal witnessed a degree of poverty and suffering among blacks that he had not seen before. Yet he also heard many white Americans profess a desire to do something about those conditions. Furthermore, the moral earnestness and optimism that Myrdal thought he saw in most white Americans (lacking in most Europeans, he said) led him to challenge them to live up to their ideals. Encouraged by the New Deal, Myrdal predicted erroneously the reconciliation between American ideals and practice. Ignoring the work of African American scholars such as Du Bois, Woodson, Charles S. Johnson and white scholars such as Herskovits, who had made the case for the strength of black culture, Myrdal adopted Frazier's and Ralph Bunche's position that African American culture was pathological.

An American Dilemma (1944) captured the attention of many white Americans on the issue of race relations, educated them on the problem of racial discrimination, and influenced political leaders, judges, and civil rights activists. But although Myrdal's ideas were durable for twenty years, Jackson points out correctly that he offered "few guidelines for the next phase of the black struggle from the passage of the 1964 Civil Rights Act and 1965 Voting Rights Act."[28]

I have a serious reservation about Jackson's splendid work. By emphasizing the importance of African American culture, he seems to suggest that a monolithic culture determines the behavior of its members. But no monolithic African American culture exists and perhaps never existed. Rather, African American cultures are so divided along regional, religious, occupational, and class lines that at this historical juncture (as Harold Cruse pointed out in the 1960s) it seems necessary to create a cultural nationalism to unify the African American groups.

Myrdal was certainly correct on some issues: as he correctly pointed out, black family, income, nutrition, housing, health, and education standards have been dependent upon opportunities in employment. And for most blacks, opportunities in employment in the new service economy, as a result of historical deprivation and present-day discrimination, are severely limited. Given the persistence of racism—however uneven—in the United States, it seems that nothing short of both a *redistribution* of wealth and an accompanying *revitalization* of African American culture can resolve satisfactorily the historical contradiction between ideals and practices.

Scholars in the history of the social science of race relations have delved into African American history in an attempt to create truly ecumenical myths. Their interest in the pioneering students of race and race relations has resulted in the resurrection of the work of an early African American sociologist who was involved in debates on the subject at the turn of the century: Monroe Nathan Work, the subject of Linda O. McMurray's *Recorder of the Black Experience* (1985).

Work's contributions to scholarship and black uplift were substantial. His biennial, publication *The Negro Year Book: A Bibliography of the Negro in Africa and America* and his early scholarly and popular articles expressed "his desire to eliminate outmoded white prejudice and to inspire black confidence." Work was also an activist. He established a National Negro Health Week; he published the *Tuskegee Lynching Report*, which contained statistics that were distributed to hundreds of newspapers; and he actively sought to increase the number of black registered voters in Macon County, Alabama. For McMurray, however, his historical significance derives not from his activism or his scholarship but from the insights "his life provides into the age in which he lived." Work was representative of Afro-American scholars who were "forced to become 'race men' in the face of the failures of white scholarship." For southern blacks, McMurray thinks, persons such as Work were "part of the rock from which the civil rights movement was hewn."[29]

Although *Recorder of the Black Experience* is a significant study, I disagree with McMurray's assessment of Work's scholarship. It is true that his scholarly articles were concise and seemed "almost devoid of interpretation," but it should be remembered that in the context of turn-of-the-century sociology his works were "scientific" attempts to undermine racism. Like Du Bois, R.R. Wright Jr., George E. Haynes, and Kelly Miller, Work believed that his discipline must shed its ties to moral philosophy and present an "objective" picture of society. Of course, recent students of the sociology of knowledge have shown that values impinge on all aspects of the social scientific enterprise; still, Work's insistence on attempting to write scientific sociology was a necessary attack on those white scholars and commentators who approached the study of blacks as if the issues were clear-cut, as if detailed statistical studies were not prerequisite for their broad conclusions.

Scholars of the history and social science of race relations should be deeply indebted to Jeffrey C. Stewart for uncovering and meticulously reconstructing in 1992 a series of extant lectures by another pioneer, the philosopher better known for his later contributions to the Harlem Renaissance than for his social scientific theorizing: Alain LeRoy Locke. The resulting book, *Race Contacts and Interracial Relations: Lectures on the Theory and Practice of Race*, offers invaluable insight into the thought of an African American intellectual on the nature of race relations during the Progressive era and on its relationship to ethnic and class relations as well. Unlike the empiricist Work, Locke was a theoretician. So fecund are these lectures with insights and hypotheses deserving further investigation and analysis that it would require a work of equal length to do justice to the collection.

Problematical for most recent scholars, however, and an indicator that he too was a prisoner of his times, is Locke's analysis of racial prejudice. Because he believed that since ancient times racial prejudice had been "automatic and instinctive," it is not surprising that Locke held what the Swedish political economist Gunnar Myrdal called a "laissez-faire, donothing" approach in reference to the potency of the law for changing race relations (Locke's works were influenced somewhat significantly by the theories of Robert Ezra Park). "It would seem," Locke remarked, "that in the majority of instances, almost as soon as there is any recognition or sense of a difference, the law springs up to help confirm it and perpetuate [the difference]." Writing in the period when the Supreme Court's decision in *Plessy v. Ferguson* had legitimized Jim Crow, Locke concluded on a fatalistic note: "One of the saddest phenomena with which the study of society can concern us is the way in which every legal, every customary, prescription accentuates and perpetuates differences [and] handicaps which would perhaps pass off as temporary accidents if they did not have the sanction and the perpetuation of the legal or the customary forms. [This is the] *stereotype function of the law*."[30]

On the relationship of race relations to class relations, Locke argued: "Race issues are only very virulent forms of class issues, because as they can be broken up into class issues they become possible of solution in society."[31] Likewise, he perceived a similarity between race relations and ethnic relations. For Locke, the relations that existed between dominant and minority groups in Europe—which were separated not by skin color but rather by speech dialects, customs, and religious faith—were the basis for group domination and exploitation. It should be noted that those of us with historical hindsight might disagree with Locke's conjoining of race and ethnicity, but there is no doubt that the views he propounded in 1916 are worthy of serious consideration.

The contributions of McMurray and Stewart are the kinds of book-length studies that African American history can bequeath to the subfield of the history of race relations social science. Needed now are new interpretations of W.E.B. Du Bois's Atlanta University publications and of Alain LeRoy Locke's forays into sociology and anthropology before the 1920s, plus studies of George Edmund Haynes, Richard R. Wright Jr., and Kelly Miller as pioneers in the early period of professional sociology. African American participation in the newly emerging social sciences from 1920 to 1930 is also terra incognita. "By the early 1920s," Stanfield wrote in 1985, "there was a noticeable void in the production of quality scholarship on the black experience relating to that done between the 1890s and 1910."[32] Popular publications such as *The Crisis* and *Opportunity: Journal of Negro Life*, however, did contain discursive articles produced by scholars. Rather than simply dismiss the 1920s as a "void," therefore, today's researchers should pay attention to the popular works of African American psychologists such as Howard H. Long, Joseph St. Clair Price, and Horace Mann Bond—especially their relationship to the skeptical stance taken by Boas and his students vis-à-vis the mental testers who were in the heyday of their influence on the general public.

Unlike those of the 1920s, the social scientific studies of African Americans published during the 1930s and 1940s have been subjected to close scrutiny by scholars (such as Stanfield, Persons, Jackson, McKee, and I). The work of E. Franklin Frazier on the African American family, which has had public policy implications, is a center of heated debate. In his timely biography *E. Franklin Frazier Reconsidered*, Anthony M. Platt—a professor of social work at California State University, Sacramento—has attempted to challenge two contradictory myths created by intellectuals since the distinguished American scholar's death in 1962. The first tale, which according to Platt is told mainly by progressives, "derives from his posthumous association with *The Negro Family: The Case for National Action*"; the progressives accept "at face value the derisive nomination of Frazier as father of the Moynihan Report." The second tale, told mainly by respected academicians, raises Frazier to "sainthood"; its narrators "return to Frazier's graduate training in Chicago but, unlike his detractors, commemorate him as a loyal and capable disciple of Robert Park and other white academics who were generous enough to recruit Afro-American students despite the prevalence of racism in academia."[33]

Platt draws on numerous archival sources—the memories and files of Frazier's colleagues, acquaintances, and friends and the heretofore undisclosed FBI and State Department files on Frazier—to reveal the complexity of and contradictions in the sociologist's life and work. Platt invites his readers to consider Frazier "as somebody who tried . . . 'to provide answers to important questions' about the persistence of racism and social inequality."[34]

Platt is adept in depicting some of the contradictions that characterize the life of the "Enfant Terrible." For example, he points out that when Frazier turned thirty-four, both parents and his sister were dead; he had cut himself off from his brother; and his wife had "found out that she could not bear children." This man "who devoted many years to studying the Afro-American family," Platt concludes, "spent his own adult life outside the conventions of a traditional or extended nuclear family. Perhaps his father's emphasis on the importance of being a self-made man also stamped Edward with the character of a loner, a person who valued independence almost to the point of isolation." Furthermore, Frazier—who challenged Melville J. Herskovits's theme that West African customs "played a decisive role in the development of Afro-American culture"—"claimed that he was of Ibo descent and he was very proud of it."[35]

Despite its flashes of brilliance, Platt's book presents certain problems. First, by anchoring Frazier's political ideology in the period between 1922 and 1927, when he was director of the Atlanta School of Social Work, Platt turns Frazier into a "militant race man." I generally associate the phrase "race man" with such persons as Marcus Garvey, Elijah Muhammed, and Malcolm X (in the middle period of his life), not with reflective integrationists like Frazier. Second, Platt's attempt to disconnect Frazier from what Charles Valentine labels the "pejorative tradition" in the culture-of-poverty debate is unconvincing. It is my contention that Frazier cannot be viewed as a postmodern man. A product of the Victorian Age and born into a family with a father who was a strong male role model, Frazier should not be regarded as a progressive on the issue of the extended nuclear family.

Furthermore, Platt does not seem to comprehend the vicissitudes of the decade in which Frazier's studies of Afro-American families were written. The 1930s were years of extreme hardship for a vast majority of the black population, as well as for a large proportion of the white population. Historical deprivation compounded by racism made the economic vulnerability of blacks especially chronic. As a member of the elite concerned with social problems emanating from the economic crisis, Frazier wanted to assist blacks in weathering the crisis and, eventually, escaping poverty. Although he was naive in believing that the escape from poverty was possible only through the establishment of strong patriarchal families, like most black intellectuals of the period Frazier placed the onus of the responsibility for bringing about concrete change on blacks themselves.

To sum up, the history of the social science of race relations has accomplished at least one goal: it has raised the issue of race in general to a level of primary concern on the agenda in the field of intellectual history. And although this subfield is dominated by historians and historically minded social scientists who have a bias—that is, they do not recognize that scholars such as Boas, Park, and Myrdal cannot be dismissed solely as either prisoners of their times or harbingers of the future—they have at least revealed the complexity of the problems those social scientists confronted and the profundity of their paradoxes. Furthermore, although the history of the social science of race relations has a long way to go toward integrating the numerous historically significant African American social scientists into their new field, it is important to remember that the work has begun. If the trend continues, the subfield will reach its goal of creating truly ecumenical "mythistory."

Notes

Full information for the sources cited here in brief may be found in the Bibliography.

Introduction

1. The variety of responses on the part of minority groups to the claims of scientific racism have been delineated in Nancy Leys Stepan and Sander L. Gilman, "Appropriating the Idioms of Science: The Rejection of Scientific Racism," in LaCapra, *The Bounds of Race*, 88-103. The first two responses of Boas may be labeled *recontextualism*; the third, *universalization*.

2. Ibid., 99.

1. Franz Uri Boas's Paradox

1. Herskovits, *Franz Boas*; Gossett, *Race*; Newby, *Jim Crow's Defense*; Higham, *Strangers in the Land*; Stocking, *Race, Culture, and Evolution*; Lieberman, "The Debate over Race"; Harris, *The Rise of Anthropological Theory*; Beardsley, "The American Scientist as Social Activist"; Diner, *In the Almost Promised Land*; Cravens, *The Triumph of Evolution*; Williams, *From a Caste to a Minority*; Hyatt, *Franz Boas—Social Activist*; Degler, *In Search of Human Nature*; Barkan, *The Retreat of Scientific Racism*; Smedley, *Race in North America*.

2. Stocking, *Race, Culture, and Evolution*, 33-34; Beardsley, "The American Scientist as Social Activist," 51; Williams, *From a Caste to a Minority*; Hyatt, *Franz Boas—Social Activist*.

3. Hankins, *The Racial Basis of Civilization*, 323.

4. George M. Fredrickson, "Reflections on the Comparative History and Sociology of Racism," 2:3, 5.

5. Hyatt, *Franz Boas—Social Activist*, 4.

6. Ibid.

7. Stocking, *Race, Culture, and Evolution*, 143.

8. Quoted in Herskovits, *Franz Boas*, 1.

9. Williams, *From a Caste to a Minority*, 34-57.

10. Stocking, *Race, Culture, and Evolution*, 189.

11. Stocking, *A Franz Boas Reader*, 220.

12. Boas, "Human Faculty as Determined by Race," 223-27.

13. Stocking, *Race, Culture and Evolution*, 163-64.

14. Quoted in Gould, *The Mismeasure of Man*, 87.

15. Boas, "Human Faculty as Determined by Race," 232.

16. Stanton, *The Leopard's Spots*.

17. Boas, "Human Faculty as Determined by Race," 316.

18. Quoted in Haller, *Outcasts from Evolution*, 178, 191; also quoted in Gould, *The Mismeasure of Man*, 116.

19. Boas, "Human Faculty as Determined by Race," 230.

20. Ibid, 242.

21. Thomas, "The Scope and Method of Folk-Psychology," 436-37.

22. Boas, "The Mind of Primitive Man," 1-11.

23. Ibid.

24. Boas, "Human Faculty as Determined by Race," 239.

25. Ibid.

26. Osofsky, *Harlem, the Making of a Ghetto*, chap. 2.

27. Marks, *Farewell—We're Good and Gone*; Grossman, *Land of Hope*; Fredrickson, *The Arrogance of Race*, 265.

28. Ovington, *Half A Man*, ix; Boas, "The Negro and the Demands of Modern Life"; and Boas, "The Real Race Problem."

29. Boas, "The Negro and the Demands of Modern Life," 86.

30. Ibid., 87.

31. Franz Boas to Edward T. Devine, Oct. 21, 1905 (Boas Papers).

32. Franz Boas to Vladimir G. Simkhovich, March 15, 1906 (Boas Papers).

33. Franz Boas to Felix Adler, Oct. 10, 1906 (Boas Papers).

34. Franz Boas to Rev. James Boddy, May 7, 1906 (Boas Papers).

35. R.R. Wright Sr. to Franz Boas, Jan. 2, 1907; Franz Boas to R.R. Wright Sr., Feb. 27, 1907 (Boas Papers).

36. Bean, "The Negro Brain," 783, 778. Bean indicated in a footnote that "the purely scientific aspect of this subject will be treated at length . . . [in] *American Journal of Anatomy*." It was; see Bean, "Some Racial Peculiarities of the Negro Brain," 353-432. Franklin P. Mall, Bean's teacher, criticized the latter work in "On Several Anatomical Characters of the Human Brain, Said to Vary According to Race and Sex with Especial Reference to the Weight of the Frontal Lobe," *American Journal of Anatomy* 9 (1909): 1-32. The prominent anatomist Burt Green Wilder also criticized Bean in "The Brain of the American Negro," *Proceedings of the First National Negro Conference* (n.d.), p. 23.

37. Bean, "The Negro Brain," 784.

38. Franz Boas to Richard Watson Gilder, Sept. 18, 1906 (Boas Papers).

39. Quoted in Hyatt, *Franz Boas—Social Activist*, 93.

40. Boas, "The Real Race Problem."

41. Boas, "Race Problems in America," 23.

42. Ibid.

43. Robert H. Lowie, review of *The Mind of Primitive Man* by Franz Boas, 830-31.

44. Boas, Foreword to Ovington, *Half A Man*, vii-viii.

45. Boas, "Human Faculty as Determined by Race," 240.

46. Hankins, *The Racial Basis of Civilization*, 323-24.

47. Brinton, "The Aims of Anthropology," 12.

48. Hyatt, *Franz Boas—Social Activist*, 79.

49. Williams, *From a Caste to a Minority*, 69-73, 84-98.

50. Park, "Education and Its Relation to the Conflict and Fusion of Cultures," 40-41.

51. Boas, "Human Faculty as Determined by Race," 226.

52. Boas, "Industries of African Negroes," 225.

53. Boas, *The Mind of Primitive Man*, 272.

54. Ibid., 274-75.

55. Brinton, *Races and Peoples*, 191-92.

56. Brinton, *The Bases of Social Relations*, 71.

57. Boas, "Human Faculty as Determined by Race," 225.

58. Boas, "What the Negro Has Done in Africa," 106-9.

59. Franz Boas to Felix Adler, Oct. 10, 1906 (Boas Papers).

60. Franz Boas to Andrew Carnegie, Nov. 30, 1906 (Boas Papers).

61. Franz Boas to George A. Plimpton, May 10, 1907 (Boas Papers).

62. W.E.B. Du Bois to Franz Boas, Oct. 11, 1905; Franz Boas to Edward T. Devine, Oct. 21, 1905 (Boas Papers).

63. Franz Boas, "The Outlook for the American Negro," 311, 316, 313.

64. Boas, "Industries of African Negroes," 223-24.

65. Ibid.

66. Ibid.

67. Franz Boas to Starr Murphy, Nov. 23, 1906 (Boas Papers).

68. Boas, "Industries of African Negroes," 219.

69. Carter G. Woodson to Franz Boas, March 17, 1920; Franz Boas to Carter G. Woodson, March 29, 1920 (Boas Papers).

70. Franz Boas to Starr Murphy, Nov. 23, 1906 (Boas Papers).

71. Jerome Dowd, *The Negro Races*, 1:5, 432, 447-48; Williams, *From a Caste to a Minority:* 35-42.

72. Tillinghast, *The Negro in Africa and America*, 96.

73. Phillips, *American Negro Slavery*, 4.

74. Eugene D. Genovese, introduction to Philips, *American Negro Slavery*, viii.

75. Du Bois, *Black Folk*, vii.

76. Quoted in McPherson, *The Abolitionist Legacy*, 345.

77. Willis Huggins to Franz Boas, Oct. 16, 1911 (Boas Papers).

78. Higham, *Strangers in the Land*, 277-86.

79. Boas, "The Problem of the American Negro," 386-87.

80. Ibid.

81. Ibid., 388-89.

82. Ibid., 390.

83. Boas, "What Is Race?" 90-91.

84. Boas, *Anthropology and Modern Life*, 18, 38, 40.

85. Fredrickson, *The Arrogance of Race*, 179.

2. Boas and the African American Intelligentsia

1. Hyatt, *Franz Boas—Social Activist*, 33-34.

2. Hoffman, *Race Traits and Tendencies of the American Negro*, pref.

3. Ibid., 312, 188.

4. Miller, Review of *Race Traits and Tendencies of the American Negro* by Frederick L. Hoffman, 11.

5. Ibid., 13.

6. Ibid., 22-23.

7. Ibid., 25, 36.

8. Lewis, *W.E.B. Du Bois*, 139.

9. Du Bois, *The Philadelphia Negro*, 5-9.

10. W.E.B. Du Bois, "The Study of Negro Problems," *Annals of the American Academy of Political and Social Science* 11 (Jan. 1898): 19.

11. Du Bois to Franz Boas, Oct. 11, 1905 (Boas Papers).

12. Franz Boas to W.E.B. Du Bois, Oct. 14, 1905 (Boas Papers).

13. "Monroe Nathan Work" (Guzman Papers).

14. Ibid.

15. Du Bois, *The Health and Physique of the Negro American*, 27.

16. Quoted in Elliott M. Rudwick, *W.E.B. Du Bois*, 123.

17. T.E. Taylor to Booker T. Washington, Sept. 4, 1915 (Washington Papers).

18. Booker T. Washington to T.E. Taylor, Sept. 14, 1915 (Washington Papers).

19. Locke, *Race Contacts and Interracial Relations*, 5.

20. Ibid., 11.

21. Ibid., 5-12.

22. Michael Winston and Rayford Logan, "George Washington Ellis," in *The Dictionary of American Negro Biography* (New York: Norton, 1982), 211-12.

23. "Some Facts of George W. Ellis" n.d. (Ellis Papers).

24. Washington, D.C., and "Kansas Newspapers" (Ellis Papers).

25. Ibid.

26. Ellis, "Psychology of American Race Prejudice," 312; see also Ellis, "The Negro in Democracy," 78; and Ellis, "Factors in the New American Race Situation," 486. Ellis was aware of Boas's innovative thinking as early as 1907; see George W. Ellis to Franz Boas, May 28, 1907 (Boas Papers).

27. Williams, *From a Caste to a Minority*.

28. Franklin, "Black Social Scientists and the Mental Testing Movement." 201-15.

29. Charles S. Johnson to Franz Boas, April 13, 1925 (Boas Papers).

30. Franz Boas to Charles S. Johnson, April 25, 1925 (Boas Papers).

31. Abram Harris to Franz Boas, June 22, 1928 (Boas Papers).

32. Charles H. Thompson to Franz Boas, June 23, 1928 (Boas Papers).

33. Franz Boas to Charles H. Thompson, July 5, 1928 (Boas Papers).

34. Howard Hale Long to Franz Boas, March 13, 1929 (Boas Papers).

35. Franz Boas to Howard Hale Long, March 18, 1929 (Boas Papers).

36. Monroe N. Work to Franz Boas, July 14, 1920; Franz Boas to Monroe N. Work, July 13, 1920 (Boas Papers).

37. Hemenway, *Zora Neal Hurston*, 88-89. The negotiations between Boas and Woodson concerning Hurston's fellowship can be found in Franz Boas to Carter G. Woodson, Nov. 18, 1926; Carter G. Woodson to Franz Boas, Nov. 23, 1926; Franz Boas to Carter G. Woodson, Dec. 7, 1926; Carter G. Woodson to Franz Boas, Feb. 17, 1927 (Boas Papers).

38. Franz Boas to Zora N. Hurston, May 3, 1927 (Boas Papers).

39. Hemenway, *Zora Neale Hurston*, 106-10.

40. Franz Boas to Zora N. Hurston, Dec. 18, 1928 (Boas Papers).

41. Zora N. Hurston to Franz Boas, Dec. 27, 1928 (Boas Papers).

42. Franz Boas to Zora N. Hurston, May 29, 1929 (Boas Papers).

43. Otto Klineberg to Franz Boas, Nov. 18, 1929 (Boas Papers).

44. Franz Boas to Zora N. Hurston, Sept. 12, 1934 (Boas Papers).

45. Franz Boas, preface to Zora Neale Hurston, *Mules and Men* (New York: Lippincott, 1935), xiii-xiv.

46. Zora N. Hurston to Franz Boas, Jan. 4, 1935 (Boas Papers).

47. Melville J. Herskovits to Franz Boas, Jan. 18, 1935 (Boas Papers).

48. Franz N. Boas to Zora N. Hurston, April 1, 1935 (Boas Papers).

49. Leonard Harris, introduction to *The Philosophy of Alain Locke: Harlem Renaissance and Beyond*, ed. Leonard Harris (Philadelphia: Temple University Press, 1989), 6.

50. Alain L. Locke to Franz Boas, Dec. 3, 1925 (Boas Papers).

51. Franz Boas to President of the American Association of University Professors, Dec. 5, 1925 (Boas Papers).

52. Alain L. Locke to Franz Boas, Dec. 14, 1925; Emmett J. Scott to Alain L. Locke, Dec. 10, 1925 (Boas Papers).

53. Carter G. Woodson to Franz Boas, Nov. 16, 1926 (Boas Papers).

54. "Memorandum: Alain Locke to Carter G. Woodson," Nov. 16, 1926 (Boas Papers).

55. Franz Boas to Carter G. Woodson, Nov. 18, 1926 (Boas Papers).

56. Carter G. Woodson to Franz Boas, Nov. 19, 1926 (Boas Papers).

56. Franz Boas to Carter G. Woodson, Nov. 23, 1926 (Boas Papers).

57. Franz Boas to Carter G. Woodson, April 30, 1923; Franz Boas to Carter G. Woodson, May 15, 1923 (Boas Papers).

58. Carter G. Woodson to Franz Boas, May 15, 1923 (Boas Papers).

59. Franz Boas to Carter G. Woodson, Nov. 18, 1926; Franz Boas to Carter G. Woodson, Nov. 22, 1926; Carter G. Woodson to Franz Boas, Feb. 17, 1927; Carter G. Woodson to Franz Boas, Feb. 24, 1927 (Boas Papers).

60. Abram L. Harris to Franz Boas, Feb. 26, 1930 (Boas Papers).

61. Abram L. Harris to Franz Boas, Oct. 9, 1936 (Boas Papers).

62. George E. Haynes to Franz Boas, Dec. 20, 1938 (Boas Papers).

3. The Myths of Africa in the Writings of Booker T. Washington

1. Gossett, *Race*; Newby, *Jim Crow's Defense*; Frederickson, *The Black Image in the White Mind*; Cravens, *The Triumph of Evolution*.

2. Gossett, *Race*; Stocking, *Race, Culture, and Evolution*; Harris, *The Rise of Anthropological Theory*; Hyatt, *Franz Boas—Social Activist*; Smedley, *Race in North America*.

3. A distinguished historian of the South African past has defined a political myth as "a tale told about the past to legitimize or discredit a regime," and a "political mythology as a cluster of such myths that reinforce one another and jointly constitute the historical element in the ideology of the regime or its rival." Thompson, *The Political Mythology of Apartheid*, 1.

4. Williams, *History of the Negro Race*, 1:109-10.

5. The great historian of African American nationalism, Wilson J. Moses, has defined "civilization" as the belief that "Africans would be uplifted and redeemed in proportion to the acceptance of European civilization": Moses, *The Wings of Ethiopia*, 102-3, 153-54.

6. For an exposition of Franz Boas's pioneering work on the African background, see Williams, "Franz Boas's Paradox," 9-17.

7. Washington, *Up from Slavery*, 218-21.

8. Ibid., 220.

9. Ibid., 223.

10. August Meier, *Negro Thought in America*, 110-14; Harlan, *Booker T. Washington: The Making of a Black Leader*, 298-99.

11. Robert E. Park, lectures from a course titled "The Negro in America," 31-32 (Park Papers).

12. Ibid.

13. Washington, *Up From Slavery*, 16.

14. Washington, *Frederick Douglass*, 5.

15. Fredrickson, *The Black Image in the White Mind*, 255.

16. Washington and Du Bois, *The Negro in the South*, 74-75.

17. Ibid., 40.

18. Washington, *The Future of the American Negro*, 6-7.

19. Washington, *Up from Slavery*, 80.

20. Ibid., 83.

21. Washington, *The Future of the American Negro*, 13-14.

22. Washington, *Up from Slavery*, 85-86.

23. Ibid., 86

24. Meier, *Negro Thought in America*, 85; Moses, *The Golden Age of Black Nationalism*, 93.

25. Washington, *Selected Speeches of Booker T. Washington*, 277.

26. Quoted in Thorough, *Booker T. Washington*, 157.

27. Washington and Du Bois, *The Negro in the South*, 20-21.

28. Franz Boas to Booker T. Washington, Nov. 30, 1904 (Boas Papers).

29. Ibid.

30. Ibid.

31. Booker T. Washington to Franz Boas, Dec. 9, 1904 (Boas Papers).

32. Hemenway, *Zora Neale Hurston*, 206-14.

33. Franz Boas to Booker T. Washington, Nov. 8, 1906; Booker T. Washington to Franz Boas, June 17, 1912 (Boas Papers).

34. Harlan, introduction to Harlan et al., *The Booker T. Washington Papers*, 1:xxxvii.

35. Quoted in McMurray, *Recorder of the Black Experience*, 60.

36. Harlan, introduction to Harlan et al., *The Booker T. Washington Papers*, 1:xxxviii.

37. "Monroe Nathan Work" (Guzman Papers).

38. Work, "An Autobiographical Sketch," Feb. 7, 1940 (Work Papers).

39. Ibid.

40. Ibid.

41. Washington, *The Story of the Negro*, 1:32, 47, 50, 58, 59, 71, 74, 75.

42. Raushenbush, *Robert E. Park*, 1-62.

43. Matthews, *Quest for an American Sociology*, 32-33.

44. Lyman, *Militarism, Imperialism, and Racial Accommodation*, xvii.

45. Quoted in Charles S. Johnson, "Robert E. Park: In Memoriam," *Sociology and Social Research* 28 (May-June, 1944): 355; Robert E. Park to Booker T. Washington, June 2, 1905 (Washington Papers).

46. Quoted in Raushenbush, *Robert E. Park*, 63.

47. Stanfield, *Philanthropy and Jim Crow*, 42.

48. Robert E. Park to Booker T. Washington, June 2, 1908 (Washington Papers).

49. Washington, *The Story of the Negro*, 5-6, 8-9.

50. Ibid., 24.

51. Ibid.

52. Quoted in Breasted, *Pioneer to the Past*, 176.

53. James H. Breasted to Booker T. Washington, April 29, 1909 (Washington Papers).

54. Booker T. Washington to James H. Breasted, May 6, 1909 (Washington Papers).

55. Washington, *Selected Speeches of Booker T. Washington*, 282.

4. W.E.B. Du Bois, George W. Ellis, and the Reconstruction of the Image of Africa

1. Du Bois, *The World and Africa*, viii.

2. Du Bois, *Dusk of Dawn*, 114-15.

3. Du Bois, *Some Efforts of American Negroes For Their Own Social Betterment*, 4-5.

4. Du Bois, "The Study of Negro Problems," *Annals of the American Academy of Political and Social Science* 11 (Jan. 1898): 11.

5. Ibid., 21; Du Bois, *The Negro in Business*, 12.

6. Franz Boas to W.E.B. Du Bois, Oct. 14, 1905 (Boas Papers).

7. Quoted in Isaacs, *The New World of Negro Americans*, 207.

8. Du Bois, *The Negro American Family*, 9.

9. Du Bois, *Efforts for Social Betterment among Negro Americans*, 10.

10. Du Bois and Dill, *Morals and Manners Among Negro Americans*, 67.

11. Du Bois, *The Negro*, 7.

12. Ibid.

13. Ibid., 19-21.

14. Ibid., 28.

15. Ibid., 28-35.

16. August Meier and Elliott Rudwick, *Black History and the Historical Profession, 1915-1980* (Urbana: Univ. of Illinois Press, 1986), 7.

17. White, *Social Thought in America*, 12.

18. Du Bois, *The Negro*, 188-89.

19. Clark Wissler to W.E.B. Du Bois, Dec. 7, 1909 (Du Bois Papers).

20. Drake, *Black Folk*, 132-37.

21. George W. Ellis, "Education in Liberia," 111-29.

22. George W. Ellis to Otis T. Mason, April 4, 1906 (Ellis Papers).

23. George W. Ellis to Franz Boas, May 28, 1907 (Ellis Papers).

24. Franz Boas to George W. Ellis, Aug. 28, 1908 (Boas Papers).

25. George W. Ellis to W.E.B. Du Bois, July 15, 1908 (Ellis Papers).

26. Walter Neale to George W. Ellis, Jan. 18, 1913; Jan. 30, 1913; April 15, 1914; and April 25, 1914 (Ellis Papers).

27. Ellis, *Negro Culture in West Africa*, 18-20.

28. Ibid., 25, 273.

29. Ibid., 273-74.

30. Ralph E. Luker, *The Social Gospel in Black and White: American Racial Reform, 1885-1912*, 34-56.

31. Ellis, *Negro Culture in West Africa*, 128, 130, 135.

32. Moses, *Alexander Crummell*, 132.

33. Ellis, *Negro Culture in West Africa*, 85-109.

34. Ibid., 109.

35. Ibid.

36. Ellis, "An Address on The Protestant Episcopal Church as a Form in Liberian Education," Dec. 8, 1909 (Ellis Papers).

37. Ellis, *Negro Culture in West Africa*, 114.

38. Ibid., 268-69.

39. Ibid., 269-270.

40. Ibid., 119-20.

41. Ibid., 124.

42. Walter Neale to George W. Ellis, Feb. 19, 1915, and Dec. 11, 1919 (Ellis Papers); W.E.B. Du Bois, Review of *Negro Culture in West Africa* by George W. Ellis, 199-200; Park, Review of *Negro Culture in West Africa* by George W. Ellis, 841-42. Present-day writers still refer to Ellis's achievements in Negro Culture in West Africa; see Peter Duignan and L.H. Gann, *The United States and Africa: A History*, 411 n. 30; and John Hope Franklin and Alfred A. Moss, Jr., *From Slavery to Freedom: A History of African Americans*, 579.

5. Robert Ezra Park and American Race and Class Relations

1. Wilson, *The Declining Significance of Race*, 153.

2. Ringer, *"We The People" and Others*, 544-54; Pettigrew, "The Changing—Not Declining—Significance of Race," 19-21; Willie, *The Caste and Class Controversy on Race and Poverty*.

3. Pinkney, *The Myth of Black Progress*, p. 97.

4. Van den Berghe, *The Ethnic Phenomenon*; and Van den Berghe, "Bringing the Beasts Back In," 777-88.

5. Degler, *In Search of Human Nature*, 189.

6. Odum, *Social and Mental Traits of the Negro*, 29.

7. Williams, *From a Caste to a Minority*, chaps. 2, 4.

8. Stanfield, *Philanthropy and Jim Crow*, 40.

9. Quoted in Harlan, *Booker T. Washington: The Wizard of Tuskegee*, 290-91.

10. Ibid., 175.

11. Ibid., 293.

12. Robert E. Park, "Principal Washington's Campaign," *Springfield* (Mass.) *Republican*, Nov. 24, 1909, p. 26.

13. Ibid., 26-28.

14. Haynes, "Conditions among Negroes in the Cities," 18-24.

15. Wright, "The Negro in Unskilled Labor," 14.

16. *Ibid.*, 122.

17. Du Bois, "The Negro in Literature," *Annals of the American Academy of Political and Social Science* 49 (Sept. 1913): 233.

18. Park, "Negro Home Life and Standards of Living," 147-63.

19. Park, "Racial Assimilation in Secondary Groups," 611-13.

20. Notes on "Southern Sentiments and Southern Policy toward the Negro, 1913" (Park Papers).

21. Unpublished notes on the Negro, 1913 (Park Papers).

22. Ibid.

23. Park, "Racial Assimilation in Secondary Groups," 614-23.

24. Unpublished notes on the Negro, 1913 (Park Papers).

25. Park, Introduction to Jesse F. Steiner, *The Japanese Invasion*, xv.

26. Park, "The Bases of Race Prejudice," 20.

27. Unpublished notes on the Negro, 1931 (Park Papers).

28. For biographical information, see Matthews, *Quest for an American Sociology*; and Raushenbush, *Robert E. Park*; and Robert E. Park, "The Nature of Race Relations," in *Race and Culture* (New York: Free Press, 1950), 116.

29. Park, *Race and Culture*, 315.

30. Warner, "American Caste and Class," 324.

31. See Jimmie Lewis Franklin, "Black Southerners, Shared Experience, and Place: A Reflection," 4-18.

32. Cox, *Caste, Class, and Race*, 476.

Conclusion

1. Smedley , *Race in North America*, 29.

Appendix: Toward an Ecumenical Mythistory

1. McNeill, *Mythistory and Other Essays*, 21.

2. Quoted in Southern, *Gunnar Myrdal and Black-White Relations*, 259.

3. See Herskovits, *Franz Boas*; Gossett, *Race*; Newby, *Jim Crow's Defense*; Higham, *Strangers in the Land*; Stocking, *Race, Culture, and Evolution*; Lieberman, "The Debate over Race"; Harris, *The Rise of Anthropological Theory*; Beardsley, "The American Scientist as Social Activist"; Diner, *In the Almost Promised Land*; Cravens, *The Triumph of Evolution*; Williams, *From a Caste to a Minority*; Hyatt, *Franz Boas— Social Activist*; Degler, *In Search of Human Nature*; Barkan, *The Retreat of Scientific Racism*; Smedley, *Race in North America*.

4. Vernon J. Williams Jr., "Franz Boas' Changing Attitudes towards Afro-Americans, 1894-1925," 81-94; Williams, "Franz Boas's Paradox," 9-17; Williams, "The Boasian Paradox, 1894-1915," 69-85; Williams, "Franz U. Boas and the Conflict between Science and Values," 7-16. See also Chapter 2.

5. Beardsley, "The American Scientist as Social Activist," 55.

6. Ibid., 53.

7. Diner, *In the Almost Promised Land*; 142-47.

8. Hyatt, *Franz Boas—Social Activist*, 33-34.

9. Ibid., 155.

10. Degler, *In Search of Human Nature*, 82.

11. Ibid., 75-80.

12. Barkan, *The Retreat of Scientific Racism*, 86.

13. Park, "Education and Its Relation to the Conflict and Fusion of Cultures, 59.

14. Stanfield, *Philanthropy and Jim Crow*, 50.

15. Lal, *The Romance of Culture in an Urban Civilization*, 154-55.

16. Lyman, *Militarism, Imperialism, and Racial Accommodation*, 107-8, xvii.

17. Kivisto, Review of *The Romance of Culture in an Urban Civilization* by Barbara Ballis Lal, 110.

18. Frazier, "Sociological Theory and Race Relations," 269.

19. Wacker, *Ethnicity, Pluralism, and Race*, 4, 57, 49.

20. Stanfield, *Philanthropy and Jim Crow*, 50.

21. Higham, *Send These to Me*, 220.

22. Persons, *Ethnic Studies at Chicago, 1905-1945*, 90.
23. McKee, *Sociology and the Race Problem*, 145-46.
24. Lyman, *Militarism, Imperialism, and Racial Accommodation*, 125.
25. Stepan and Gilman, "Appropriating the Idioms of Science," 99.
26. Jackson, *Gunnar Myrdal and America's Conscience*.
27. Ibid., 313.
28. Ibid., 320.
29. McMurray, *Recorder of the Black Experience*, 109.
30. Locke, *Race Contacts and Interracial Relations*, 49.
31. Ibid., 7.
32. Stanfield, *Philanthropy and Jim Crow*, 54.
33. Platt, *E. Franklin Frazier Reconsidered*, 2.
34. Ibid., 7.
35. Ibid., 14, 16.

Bibliography

Manuscript Collections

Franz Boas Papers. American Philosophical Society, Philadelphia, Pa.
George W. Ellis Papers. Chicago Historical Society, Chicago, Ill.
Booker T. Washington Papers. Library of Congress, Washington, D.C.
Monroe N. Work Papers. Tuskegee Institute, Tuskegee, Ala.
Jessie P. Guzman Papers. Tuskegee Institute, Tuskegee, Ala.
Robert E. Park Papers. University of Chicago, Chicago, Ill.

Books and Articles

Aptheker, Herbert, ed. *The Correspondence of W.E.B. Du Bois*. 3 vols. Amherst: Univ. of Massachusetts Press, 1973-78.

Barkan, Elazar. *The Retreat of Scientific Racism: Changing Concepts of Race in Britain and the United States between the World Wars*. Cambridge: Cambridge Univ. Press, 1992.

Bean, Robert Bennett. "The Negro Brain." *Century Illustrated Monthly Magazine* 72 (1906).

———. "Some Racial Peculiarities of the Negro Brain." *American Journal of Anatomy* 5 (1906): 353-432.

Beardsley, Edward H. "The American Scientist as Social Activist: Franz Boas, Burt G. Wilder, and the Cause of Racial Justice, 1900-1915." *Isis*, March 1973.

Boas, Franz. *Anthropology and Modern Life*. New York: Norton, 1928.

———. Foreword to *Half A Man: The Status of the Negro in New York*, by Mary White Ovington. New York: Longmans, Green, 1915.

———. "Human Faculty as Determined by Race." In *A Franz Boas Reader*, ed. George W. Stocking Jr. Chicago: Univ. of Chicago Press, 1974.

———. "Industries of African Negroes." *Southern Workman* 38 (April 1909): 217-29.

———. "The Mind of Primitive Man." *Journal of American Folk-Lore* 14 (Jan.-March 1901): 1-11.

———. *The Mind of Primitive Man*. New York: Macmillan, 1911.

———. "The Negro and the Demands of Modern Life." *Charities* 15 (7 Oct. 1905): 85-88.

———. "The Outlook for the America Negro." In *A Franz Boas Reader*, ed. George W. Stocking Jr. Chicago: Univ. of Chicago Press, 1974.

———. "The Problem of the American Negro." *Yale Quarterly Review* 10 (Jan. 1921): 384-95.

————. "Race Problems in America." In *A Franz Boas Reader*, ed. George W. Stocking Jr. Chicago: Univ. of Chicago Press, 1974.

————. "The Real Race Problem." *The Crisis* 7 (Dec. 1910).

————. "What Is Race?" *The Nation* 28 (Jan. 1925): 89-91.

————. "What the Negro Has Done in Africa." *Ethical Record* 5 (March 1904): 106-9.

Breasted, Charles. *Pioneer to the Past: The Story of James Henry Breasted, Archaeologist*. New York: Scribner, 1943.

Brinton, Daniel G. "The Aims of Anthropology." *Proceedings of the American Association for the Advancement of Science* 44 (Dec. 1895): 1-17.

————. *The Bases of Social Relations*. New York: Putnam, 1902.

————. *Races and Peoples: Lectures on the Science of Ethnology*. New York: N.D.C. Hodges, 1890.

Childs, John Brown. *Leadership, Conflict, and Cooperation in Afro-American Social Thought*. Philadelphia: Temple Univ. Press, 1989.

Cox, Oliver C. *Caste, Class, and Race: A Study of Social Dynamics*. New York: Doubleday, 1948.

Cravens, Hamilton. *The Triumph of Evolution: American Scientists and the Hereditary-Environmentalist Controversy, 1900-1941*. Philadelphia: Univ. of Pennsylvania Press, 1978.

Dowd, Jerome. *The Negro Races*. 2 vols. New York: Macmillan, 1907-14.

Degler, Carl N. *In Search of Human Nature: The Decline and Revival of Darwinism in American Social Thought*. New York: Oxford Univ. Press, 1991.

Diner, Hasia R. *In the Almost Promised Land: Jews and Blacks*. Westport, Conn.: Greenwood Press, 1977.

Drake, St. Clair. *Black Folk, Here and There: An Essay in History and Anthropology*. 2 vols. Los Angeles: Center for Afro-American Studies, Univ. of California, Los Angeles, 1987-91.

Duigman, Peter and L.H. Gann. *The United States and Africa: A History*. Cambridge: Cambridge Univ. Press, 1984.

Du Bois, W.E.B. *Black Folk: Then and Now*. New York: Henry Holt, 1939.

————. *Dusk of Dawn: An Essay Toward an Autobiography of a Race Concept*. 1940. Rpt. New York: Schocken Books, 1968.

————, ed. *Efforts for Social Betterment among Negro Americans: Report of a Social Study Made by Atlanta University under the Patronage of the Trustees of the John F. Slater Fund; Together with the Proceedings of the 14th Annual Conference for the Study of Negro Problems*. Atlanta: Atlanta Univ. Press, 1909.

————, ed. *The Health and Physique of the Negro American: Report of a Social Study Made under the Direction of Atlanta University; Together with the Proceedings of the Eleventh Conference for the Study of Negro Problems*. Atlanta: Atlanta Univ. Press, 1906.

————. *The Negro*. 1915. Rpt. New York: Oxford Univ. Press., 1970.

————, ed. *The Negro American Family: Report of a Social Study Made Principally by the College Classes of 1909 and 1910 of Atlanta University, under the Patronage of the Trustees of the John F. Slater Fund; Together with the Proceedings of the 13th Annual Conference for the Study of Negro Problems*. Atlanta: Atlanta Univ. Press, 1908.

————, ed. *The Negro in Business: Report of a Social Study Made under the Direction of Atlanta University; Together with the Proceedings of the Fourth Conference for the Study of Negro Problems*. Atlanta: Atlanta Univ. Press, 1899.

————. *The Philadelphia Negro: A Social Study*. 1899. Rpt. New York: Schocken Books, 1967.

————. Review of *Race Traits and Tendencies of the American Negro* by Frederick L. Hoffman. *Annals of the American Academy of Political and Social Science* 9 (Jan. 1897): 127-33.

————, ed. *Some Efforts of American Negroes for Their Own Social Betterment: Report of an Investigation under the Direction of Atlanta University; Together with the Proceedings of the Third Conference for the Study of Negro Problems*. Atlanta: Atlanta Univ. Press, 1898.

————. Review of *Negro Culture in West Africa* by George W. Ellis. Crisis 5 (Feb. 1915): 199-200.

————. "The Study of the Negro Problems." *Annals of the American Academy of Political and Social Science* 11 (Jan. 1898): 1-19.

————. *The World and Africa: An Inquiry into the Part Which Africa Has Played in World History*. New York: International, 1946.

Du Bois, W.E.B., and Augustus Granville Dill, eds. *Morals and Manners among Negro Americans: Report of a Social Study Made by Atlanta University under the Patronage of the Trustees of the John F. Slater Fund; With the Proceedings of the 18th Annual Conference for the Study of the Negro Problem*. Atlanta: Atlanta Univ. Press, 1914.

Eckberg, Douglass L. *Intelligence and Race*. New York: Praeger, 1979.

Ellis, George W. "Education in Liberia." *Report of the Commissioner of Education*. Washington, D.C.: 1905.

————. "Factors in the New American Race Situation." *Journal of Race Development* 8 (April 1917).

————. *Negro Culture in West Africa: A Study of the Negro Group of Vai-Speaking People with Its Own Invented Alphabet and Written Language*. New York: Neale, 1914.

————. "The Negro in Democracy." *Journal of Race Development* 7 (July 1916).

————. "Psychology of American Race Prejudice." *Journal of Race Development* 6 (Jan. 1915).

Franklin, John Hope, and Alfred A. Moss Jr. *From Slavery to Freedom: A History of African Americans*. New York: McGraw-Hill, 1994.

Franklin, Vincent P. "Black Social Scientists and the Mental Testing Movement, 1920-1940." In *Black Psychology*, 2d ed., ed. Reginald L. Jones. New York: Harper & Row, 1980.

Frazier, E. Franklin. "Sociological Theory and Race Relations." *American Sociological Review* 12 (June 1947): 265-71.

Fredrickson, George M. "Reflections on the Comparative History and Sociology of Racism. In *American Studies in Southern Africa: Symposium Proceedings*, Pretoria: United States Information Service, 1993.

————. *The Arrogance of Race: Historical Perspectives on Slavery, Racism, and Social Inequality*. Middletown, Conn.: Wesleyan University Press, 1988.

————. *The Black Image in the White Mind: The Debate on Afro-American Character and Destiny, 1817-1914*. New York: Harper & Row, 1971.

Genovese, Eugene D. "Introduction." In *American Negro Slavery* by Ulrich B. Phillips. Baton Rouge: Louisiana State Univ. Press, 1966.

Gossett, Thomas F. *Race: The History of an Idea in America*. Dallas, Tex.: Southern Methodist Univ. Press, 1963.

Gould, Stephen Jay. *The Mismeasure of Man*. New York: Norton, 1981.

Grossman, James R. *Land of Hope: Chicago, Black Southerners, and the Great Migration*. Chicago: Univ. of Chicago Press, 1989.

Haller, John S., Jr. *Outcasts from Evolution: Scientific Attitudes toward Race in America, 1815-1900*. Urbana: Univ. of Illinois Press, 1971.

Hankins, Frank H. *The Racial Basis of Civilization*. New York: Knopf, 1926.

Harlan, Louis R. *Booker T. Washington: The Making of a Black Leader, 1856-1901*. New York: Oxford Univ. Press, 1972.

———. *Booker T. Washington: The Wizard of Tuskegee*, 1901-1915. New York: Oxford Univ. Press, 1983.

Harlan, Louis R., et al., eds. *The Booker T. Washington Papers*. 14 vols. Urbana: Univ. of Illinois Press, 1972-89.

Harris, Leonard, ed. *The Philosophy of Alain Locke: Harlem Renaissance and Beyond*. Philadelphia: Temple Univ. Press, 1989.

Harris, Marvin. *The Rise of Anthropological Theory: A History of Theories of Culture*. New York: Crowell, 1968.

Haynes, George E. "Conditions among Negroes in the Cities." *Annals of the American Academy of Political and Social Science* 49 (Sept. 1913): 18-24.

Hemenway, Robert E. *Zora Neale Hurston: A Literary Biography*. Urbana: Univ. of Illinois Press, 1972.

Herskovits, Melville J. *Franz Boas: The Science of Man in the Making*. New York: Scribner, 1953.

Higham, John. *Send These to Me: Immigrants in Urban America*. Rev. ed. Baltimore, Md.: Johns Hopkins Univ. Press, 1984.

———. *Strangers in the Land: Patterns of American Nativism*, 1860-1925. Brunswick, N.J.: Rutgers Univ. Press, 1966.

Hoffman, Frederick L. *Race Traits and Tendencies of the American Negro*. American Economic Association, 1896.

Hurston, Zora Neale. *Mules and Men*. New York: Lippincott, 1935.

Hyatt, Marshall. *Franz Boas—Social Activist: The Dynamics of Ethnicity*. New York: Greenwood Press, 1990.

Isaacs, Harold R. *The New World of Negro Americans*. New York: Viking Press, 1964.

Jackson, Walter A. *Gunnar Myrdal and America's Conscience: Social Engineering and Racial Liberalism, 1938-1987*. Chapel Hill: Univ. of North Carolina Press, 1991.

Jensen, Arthur. *Bias in Mental Testing*. London: Methuen, 1980.

Johnson, Charles S. "Robert E. Park: In Memorium." *Sociology and Social Research* 28 (May-June-June, 1944): 354-56.

Jones, Reginald L., ed. *Black Psychology*. 2d. ed. New York: Harper & Row, 1980.

Kamin, Leon J. *The Science and Politics of IQ*. Harmondsworth: Penguin Books, 1977.

Kivisto, Peter. Review of *The Romance of Culture in an Urban Civilization: Robert E. Park on Race and Ethnic Relations in Cities*, by Barbara Ballis Lal. *Journal of American Ethnic History* 12 (Fall 1992): 109-10.

LaCapra, Dominick, ed. *The Bounds of Race: Perspectives on Hegemony and Resistance*. Ithaca, N.Y.: Cornell Univ. Press, 1991.

Lal, Barbara Ballis. *The Romance of Culture in an Urban Civilization: Robert E. Park on Race and Ethnic Relations in the Cities*. London: Routledge, 1990.

Lewis, David Levering. *W.E.B. Du Bois: The Biography of a Race*, 1868-1919. New York: Norton, 1993.

Lieberman, Leonard. "The Debate over Race: A Study in the Sociology of Knowledge." *Phylon* 29 (Summer 1968): 127-41.

Locke, Alain LeRoy. *Race Contacts and Interracial Relations: Lectures on the Theory and Practice of Race.* Ed. and intro. Jeffrey C. Stewart. Washington, D.C.: Howard Univ. Press, 1992.

Lowie, Robert H. Review of *The Mind of Primitive Man* by Franz Boas. *American Journal of Sociology* 17 (May 1912): 830-31.

Luken, Ralph E. *The Social Gospel in Black and White: American Racial Reform, 1885-1912.* Chapel Hill: Univ. Of North Carolina Press, 1991.

Lyman, Stanford M. *Militarism, Imperialism, and Racial Accommodation: An Analysis and Interpretation of the Early Writings of Robert E. Park.* Fayetteville: Univ. of Arkansas Press, 1992.

McKee, James B. *Sociology and the Race Problem: The Failure of a Perspective.* Urbana: Univ. of Illinois Press, 1993.

McMurray, Linda O. *Recorder of the Black Experience: A Biography of Monroe Nathan Work.* Baton Rouge: Louisiana State Univ. Press, 1985.

McNeill, William H. *Mythistory and Other Essays.* Chicago: Univ. of Chicago Press, 1986.

McPherson, James. *The Abolitionist Legacy: From Reconstruction to the NAACP.* Princeton, N.J.: Princeton Univ. Press, 1975.

Mall, Franklin. "On Several Anatomical Characters of the Human Brain, Said to Vary According to Race and Sex with Especial Reference to the Weight of the Frontal Lobe." *American Journal of Anatomy* 9 (1909): 1-32.

Marks, Carole. Farewell—*We're Good and Gone: The Great Black Migration.* Bloomington: Indiana Univ. Press, 1989.

Matthews, Fred H. *Quest for an American Sociology: Robert E. Park and the Chicago School.* Montreal: McGill-Queen's Univ. Press, 1977.

Meier, August. *Negro Thought in America, 1880-1915: Racial Ideologies in the Age of Booker T. Washington.* Ann Arbor: Univ. of Michigan Press, 1963.

Meier, August and Elliott Rudwick. *Black History and the Historical Profession*, 1915-1980 Urbana: Univ. Of Illinois Press, 1986.

Miller, Kelly. Review of *Race Traits and Tendencies of the American Negro* by Frederick L. Hoffman. Occasional Paper No. 1, American Negro Academy, 1897.

Moses, Wilson J. *Alexander Crummell: A Study of Civilization and Discontent.* New York: Oxford University Press, 1989.

———. *The Golden Age of Black Nationalism.* 1978. Rpt. New York: Oxford University Press, 1988.

———. *The Wings of Ethiopia: Studies in African-American Life and Letters.* Ames: Iowa State Univ. Press, 1990.

Newby, Idus A. *Jim Crow's Defense: Anti-Negro Thought in America, 1909-1930.* Baton Rouge: Louisiana State Univ. Press, 1965.

Odum, Howard W. *Social and Mental Traits of the Negro.* New York: Columbia Univ. Press, 1910.

Osofsky, Gilbert. *Harlem, the Making of a Ghetto: Negro New York, 1890-1930.* New York: Harper & Row, 1963.

Ovington, Mary White. *Half a Man: The Status of the Negro in New York.* New York: Longmans, Green, 1915.

Park, Robert E. "The Bases of Race Prejudice." *Annals of the American Academy of Political and Social Science* 140 (Nov. 1928): 11-20.

————. "Education and Its Relation to the Conflict and Fusion of Cultures: With Special Reference to the Problems of the Immigrant, the Negro, and Missions." *Publications of the American Sociological Society* 13 (Dec. 1918): 40-60.

————. Introduction to *The Japanese Invasion*, by Jesse F. Steiner. New York: McClurg, 1917.

————. "Negro Home Life and Standards of Living." *Annals of the American Academy of Political and Social Science* 49 (Sept. 1913): 147-63.

————. *Race and Culture: Essays in the Sociology of Contemporary Man*. New York: Free Press, 1950.

————. "Racial Assimilation in Secondary Groups: With Particular Reference to the Negro." *American Journal of Sociology* 19 (March 1914): 607-23.

————. Review of Negro Culture in West Africa by George W. Ellis, *American Journal of Sociology* 20 (May 1915): 841-42.

Persons, Stow. *Ethnic Studies at Chicago, 1905-45*. Urbana: Univ. of Illinois Press, 1987.

Pettigrew, T.F. "The Changing—Not Declining—Significance of Race." *Contemporary Sociology*, First Quarter 1980, pp. 19-21.

Phillips, Ulrich B. *American Negro Slavery: A Survey of the Supply, Employment, and Control of Negro Labor as Determined by the Plantation Regime*. 1918. Rpt. Baton Rouge: Louisiana State Univ. Press, 1966.

Pinkney, Alphonso. *The Myth of Black Progress*. Cambridge: Cambridge Univ. Press, 1984.

Platt, Anthony M. *E. Franklin Frazier Reconsidered*. New Brunswick, N.J.: Rutgers Univ. Press, 1991.

Raushenbush, Winifred. *Robert E. Park: Biography of a Sociologist*. Durham, N.C.: Duke Univ. Press, 1975.

Ringer, Benjamin B. *"We The People" and Others*. London: Methuen, 1983.

Rudwick, Elliott M. *W.E.B. Du Bois: A Study in Minority Leadership*: Philadelphia: Univ. of Pennsylvania Press, 1961.

Smedley, Audrey. *Race in North America: Origin and Evolution of a Worldview*. Boulder, Colo.: Westview Press, 1993.

Southern, David W. *Gunnar Myrdal and Black-White Relations: The Use and Abuse of an American Dilemma, 1944-1969*. Baton Rouge: Louisiana State Univ. Press, 1987.

Stanfield, John H. *Philanthropy and Jim Crow in American Social Science*. Westport, Conn.: Greenwood Press, 1985.

Stanton, William R. *The Leopard's Spots: Scientific Attitudes toward Race in America, 1815-1859*. Chicago: Univ. of Chicago Press, 1960.

Stepan, Nancy L. *The Idea of Race in Science*. Hamden, Conn.: Archon Books, 1982.

Stocking, George W., Jr., ed. *A Franz Boas Reader: The Shaping of American Anthropology, 1883-1911*. Chicago: Univ. Of Chicago Press, 1974.

————. *Race, Culture, and Evolution: Essays in the History of Anthropology*. New York: Free Press, 1968.

Taylor, Howard F. *The IQ Game*. Brighton: Harvester Press, 1981.

Thomas, William I. "The Scope and Method of Folk-Psychology." *American Journal of Sociology* 1 (Nov. 1895): 434-63.

Thompson, Leonard M. *The Political Mythology of Apartheid*. New Haven, Conn.: Yale Univ. Press, 1985.

Thornborough, Emma Lou, ed. *Booker T. Washington*. Englewood Cliffs, N.J.: Prentice-Hall, 1969.

Tillinghast, Joseph A. *The Negro in Africa and America*. New York: Macmillan, 1902.

Van den Berghe, Pierre L. "Bringing the Beasts Back In: Toward a Biosocial Theory of Aggression." American Sociological Review, Dec. 1974, pp. 777-88.

———. *The Ethnic Phenomenon*. New York: Elsevier, 1981.

Wacker, R. Fred. *Ethnicity, Pluralism, and Race: Race Relations Theory in America before Myrdal*. Westport, Conn.: Greenwood Press, 1981.

Warner, W. Lloyd. "American Caste and Class." *American Journal of Sociology* 41 (Sept. 1936): 234-37.

Washington, Booker T. *Frederick Douglass*. 1907. Rpt. New York: Haskell House, 1968.

———. *The Future of the American Negro*. 1899. Rpt. New York: Haskell House, 1968.

———. *Selected Speeches of Booker T. Washington*. Ed. E. Washington. Garden City, N.Y.: Doubleday, Doran, 1932.

———. *The Story of the Negro: The Rise of the Race from Slavery*. 2 vols. 1909. Rpt. New York: Peter Smith, 1940.

———. *Up from Slavery*. 1901. Rpt. New York: Penguin Books, 1986.

Washington, Booker T., and W.E.B. Du Bois. *The Negro in the South: His Economic Progress in Relation to His Moral and Religious Development*. 1907. Rpt. New York: Carol, 1970.

White, Morton. *Social Thought in America: The Revolt against Formalism*. Boston: Beacon Press, 1957.

Wilder, Burt Green. "The Brain of the American Negro." *Proceedings of the First National Negro conference* (n.d.): 1-23.

Williams, George Washington. *History of the Negro Race, 1619 to 1880: Negroes as Slaves, as Soldiers, and as Citizens*. 1883. Rpt. New York: Bergman, 1968.

Williams, Vernon J., Jr. "The Boasian Paradox, 1894-1915," *Afro-Americans in New York Life and History* 16 (July 1992): 69-85.

———. "Franz Boas' Changing Attitudes towards Afro-Americans, 1894-1925." *The Bicentennial of the U.S. Constitution*, ed. by Earl S. Davis. New York: New York University Institute of Afro-American Affairs, 1988.

———."Franz Boas's Paradox." *The Griot: The Journal of Black Heritage* 10 (Fall 1991): 9-17.

———. "Franz U. Boas and the Conflict between Science and Values, 1894-1915." *American Philosophical Association Newsletter on Philosophy and the Black Experience* 92 (Spring 1993): 7-16.

———. *From a Caste to a Minority: Changing Attitudes of American Sociologists toward Afro-Americans, 1896-1945*. Westport, Conn.: Greenwood Press, 1989.

Willie, Charles Vert, ed. *The Caste and Class Controversy on Race and Poverty: Round Two of the Willie/Wilson Debate*. Dix Hill, N.Y.: General Hall, 1989.

Wilson, William J. *The Declining Significance of Race*. Chicago: Univ. of Chicago Press, 1978.

Winston, Michael, and Rayford Logan. "George Washington Ellis." In *Dictionary of American Negro Biography*. New York: Norton, 1982.

Wright, R.R., Jr. "The Negro in Unskilled Labor." *Annals of the American Academy of Political and Social Science* 49 (Sept. 1913): 19-27.

Index

100 Percent Americanism, 33

abolitionists, 58
Achimota Prince of Wales College and School: Aggrey at, 65
Adams, Romanzo, 89
Adler, Felix, 19, 27
Africa: African Americans in, 81; Aggrey in, 65; ancestry in, 1-2, 20, 25-34, 40-41, 64, 71-75, 77, 84; blacks in, 26-28, 32, 34, 56, 60, 75-76, 81; thoughts on, of Boas, 26-30, 32-34, 41, 66, 73-75, 102, 106, 121n. 6 (56); Breasted in, 71-72; Central, 75; Christianity in, 81, 83; culture of, 26-27, 29-30, 67, 76-78, 100, 115; and Du Bois (W.E.B.), 73-77; exploitation of, by Europe, 56, 69, 80; negroes in, 26-30, 32, 34, 55, 59, 63, 66, 74-75, 80-84; nexus between, and the United States, 74-75; and Park (Robert), 69, 100; race mixture in, 26, 71; slavery in, 74-75; Washington in, 2, 69-72; and Work, 67; West, 26, 72, 75, 79, 81, 84, 90, 115
African American "Civilizationist" ideology, 82
African American equipotentiality, 4, 20, 106
African American nationalism, 72
African American studies, 77
African Americans: in Africa, 81; assimilation of, 5, 7, 88, 94, 100; and Boas, 8-9, 17, 20, 28-30, 32-34, 36-37, 40, 44, 46-48, 53, 104-107; capabilities of, 4-6, 9, 23, 54, 62, 85, 92, 108; civil rights of, 42; class structure among, 40-41, 46; cranial capacity of, 42, 106; cultural identity of, 30; culture of, 1, 5, 34-35, 39, 50, 111-2, 115; "defective ancestry" of, 5, 9, 48, 106; demographic shift of, 3, 16; and Du Bois (W.E.B.), 40, 73, 75; equality for, 58, 101; ethnic identity of, 101; extinction of, 37-38, 40, 60; and Frazier, 115; history of, 27, 32, 54, 56, 73, 75, 85; intellectuals and leaders among, 1-2, 6, 28, 37, 39, 41-42, 44-46, 48, 53-56, 96, 100, 105, 111-4, 116; and Myrdal, 111; myth of homogeneity of, 3, 9, 39, 43, 87, 110; in mythistory, 103, 112; and Park (Robert), 69, 92, 108-10; physical characteristics of, 94; racial inferiority of, 46; racial stereotyping of, 29; racial traits of, 34, 38, 87; during Reconstruction, 61; retention of African cultural mannerisms by, 48, 74, 78, 100, 108-9; and the Second Reconstruction, 36; socioeconomic status of, 5-6, 24, 101, 110; in the Southern United States, 58-59, 61, 69, 89, 94; study of, 114; at the Tuskegee Normal and Industrial Institute, 71; in the United States, 7, 9, 16, 27, 39, 48, 89-90, 92, 104, 108-9; uplift of, 1-2, 28, 39-40, 53, 59, 87, 94, 97-98; and van der Veer Quick, 48; whites' relations with, 54, 59, 94, 98. *See also* blacks; negroes